DISABLE THE LABEL

Never Limit The Potential of a Child

Comments from Our Training Participants

What you taught us was that childhood trauma and suffering does not provide us with an excuse for our problems. It gives the origins of our problems but does not relieve us of the responsibility to understand and to improve ourselves. Do not blame those from the past, but use the insight to refocus on the good effects to free ourselves from its harmful ones. What a wonderful message.

As case managers, we read the files and see the kids but we don't always know the truth of how they feel.

As I reflect on my learning, I am confident that I have grown both personally and professionally. The experiences and skills that I have learned will continue to impact my work and practice with others. This was such a valuable experience.

The best training is hearing from foster youth and their journey in foster care.

This is the best training I have been to. Derek Clark gives us hope when sometimes as foster parents we see No Hope.

This training has opened my eyes to help the angry little boy we have in our home now.

I learned about the Response-Based Research Therapy and how childhood responses to trauma are manifesting in very similar behaviors to ADHD, ADD and Reactive Attachment Disorder. I am inspired.

I felt captivated the entire time. Thank you for reminding me as a social worker why I do this work and reminding me not to give up on any kid.

DISABLE THE LABEL

Never Limit The Potential of a Child

Derek Clark & Shelly Bonnah

DISABLE THE LABEL

First edition published in 2012.

ISBN: 978-0-615-66739-3

Acknowledgements

We would like to acknowledge two former youth in care, Katherine McParland and Shane Dobratz, for their contributions to this book. We are proud to honor their ongoing commitment toward training professionals to work more effectively in preserving the dignity of children and youth in the foster care system.

About the Authors

SHELLY BONNAH, MA., is a foster parent, a registered counselor, and the Chief Operating Officer/Clinical Director for a social service organization in British Columbia, Canada. Shelly is also an instructor of a Diploma program in Brief Systemic Family Therapy training and a consultant with the Centre for Response-Based Practice, which is an organization that guides research, development, and the application of Response-Based ideas. Together with her husband and children, Shelly has challenged the traditional boundaries of 'family' through their experiences of providing a home to more than twenty children and youth over a period of fifteen years. Shelly is the author of *Profiles of Resistance; A Response-Based Approach with Youth in Care.*

DEREK CLARK knows first hand about coping with adversity and overcoming hardship. His 13 years in the foster care system reflect a life of labels, humiliation, aggression, emotional distress and anxiety. Derek has experienced a life of fear, rejection, and mislabeling. Having suffered unthinkable child abuse, abandonment and emotional distress, he has never been held back from accomplishing what he set his heart and mind to.

Derek is now an inspiring motivational speaker, trainer and the author of *Never Limit Your Life* and the award winning *I Will Never Give Up* book series. He is also an Ambassador for the Foster Care Alumni of America and has been a featured foster care expert on Headline News/CNN. Derek is married and has 4 children, and has turned his situation from a victim to a victor, equipping him with the wisdom and the will to never give up.

TABLE OF CONTENTS

Introduction

This book has evolved from the trenches; a sharing of knowledge and experiences from a child within the foster care system, joined by a foster parent who is also a counselor working for kids in the system.
(Derek Clark & Shelly Bonnah)

WHO AM I & Where Do I Belong may be the private question influencing the public behavior of many children and youth in the foster care system. As professionals in the social service sector, we will explore how children and youth who are navigating the foster care system in search of a sense of belonging have grappled with this question. We will also describe how young people can be viewed, both positively and negatively, through the eyes of adults who often know them only through a short window of time. With the introduction of Response-Based ideas, we are contesting many commonly adopted orientations that pathologize, minimize, and ultimately harm children and youth. Best practices—ethical practices—must include the heightened awareness of our language customs in the social service field and must have a solid foundation rooted in our knowledge of loss, grief and traumatic experiences.

Our Motivation and Orientation

AS CAREGIVERS and professionals working for youth in the foster care system, we frequently gather in living rooms, classrooms, and boardrooms to review our practices and strive toward improving the lives of kids in foster care. Similarly, foster kids are gathered disproportionately inside the justice system and are taking psychotropic medication at rates approximately 60% higher than that of kids in the general population (Lambe, 2009). These challenges are not revelations and this book will not hold all of the answers. What is offered instead is an honest view of a child's experience growing up in the foster care system through his adult perspective, and a framework for professionals to view those experiences. Our belief is that when the adults who touch the lives of children and youth in the child welfare system collectively respond to them differently, the system itself can profoundly change.

Derek Clark & Shelly Bonnah

AN INTIMATE view into the thoughts, emotions and actions of Derek Clark's journey through childhood and foster care will answer questions that many professionals working with kids in care may not have the opportunity to ask. Although he grew up angry, violent, and rejecting of most adults in his life—Derek speaks openly about the fundamental elements that made a difference to his eventual success. He is now a motivational speaker to both youth and adult audiences, the inspirational author of *Never Limit Your Life* and the award winning *I Will Never Give Up* book series, and he is also a successful singer/ songwriter. Throughout this book, Derek will share an honest perspective regarding his 13 years in the San Francisco bay area foster care system.

Shelly Bonnah, MA., is a foster parent, a family therapist and the Chief Operating Officer for a social service agency providing support to children and youth in care. She has often tackled the challenges of anger, violence and rejection from a different vantage point than Derek. These troubling behaviors are thrown into the center between two people who are attempting to form a relationship, sometimes making it virtually impossible to see one another through the chaos. Her adaptation of the Response-Based approach, together with Dr. Allan Wade, has made it specific and applicable to youth in care and offers a way for adults to understand, orient themselves, and respond differently to the loss, grief and traumatic experiences that children and youth often endure before, during and after government care.

Although we have written this book collaboratively, we come from very different backgrounds and our voices carry uniquely different messages. For this reason, we have identified our writing in parenthesis throughout the book.

A Response-Based Approach

[Shelly] MISHANDLED SEPARATIONS are commonplace with children and youth who are removed from their homes, sometimes numerous times once they are in the foster system. "Consequently, youth living in this type of transient lifestyle over sustained periods of time are pre-conditioned to guard themselves with an understandable unwillingness to interact, integrate, or become emotionally connected to peers and caregivers" (Lambe, 2009, p. 12). Those involved with youth in care have frequent choice-points when responding to youth behavior, as child and youth behavior tends to vary quite radically depending on the environment and how they are responding the individuals around them. Psychiatric interventions, such as physical and chemical restraints may be recommended and employed as treatment strategies for a DSM-IV diagnosis such as ADHD, depression, and attachment disorder. Through the application of a Response-Based approach to the experiences of youth in care, an evolved understanding of the internal experience of these children becomes possible. This new understanding can begin to challenge both social responses and the accepted professional discourse that pathologizes behavior with labels, disorders and chemical 'treatment'. Response-Based therapy, described by Dr. Allan Wade, is:

...the development of a specific interviewing practice and the modification of practices developed in the brief, systemic, solution-focused, narrative and feminist approaches. We focus not on treating effects but on elucidating individuals' physical, emotional, mental and spiritual responses to specific acts of violence and other forms of oppression and adversity. Certain responses – often the very problem itself – become intelligible as forms of resistance that point to 'symptoms of chronic mental wellness' (Wade, 2007, pp. 8-9).

The details of responses, including resistance, consist of the physical, emotional, mental, relational and spiritual processes that run parallel to that which is easily observable. A progressive understanding is gained through eliciting the often-concealed yet ever-present resistance that serves to preserve the dignity of a young person who may be faced with dignity-stripping circumstances.

Working to Make a Difference: How We Are Doing

OUR PRIMARY goal is to create a useful resource for professionals working for children and youth in the foster care system. With the possibility of understanding the behavior(s) shown by children and youth differently, there is opportunity to respond to them in ways that will create more positive outcomes. We can be both practical and ambitious: this book may not change the system or the government's way of providing care to kids in our society *but* it is imminently critical that we collectively find solutions to how we are caring for our most vulnerable youth. The kids in the system overwhelmingly require the adults who work for the system to change because youth in care are twice as likely to:

1. Drop out of high school

2. Enter the Adult Welfare System

3. Be underemployed
   (Youth in Care Canada, 2012)

Furthermore, statistics clearly indicate that the outcomes for youth in the foster care system are not meeting the objectives of the professionals who are commissioned to care for them. The facts, as below, are clear: neither the kids are safe nor are the professionals satisfied.

Child Abuse and Neglect Statistics

ALTHOUGH THE U.S is ranked 1st in gross domestic product globally, it is:

- 20th of 21 among developed nations based on overall child well-being, and
- 25th of 27 among developed nations based on the rate of child deaths from abuse and neglect.

How many children are abused and neglected in the U.S.?

- 6.0 million children were referred to Child Protective Services (CPS).
- 3.3. Million children were investigated for maltreatment by CPS,
- 825,000 children were determined to be victims of abuse or neglect.

What type of maltreatment did these children suffer?

- 78.3% were victims of neglect.
- 17.8% were victims of physical abuse.
- 9.5% were victims of sexual abuse
- 7.6% were victims of psychological abuse.

How many children in the U.S. died from abuse and neglect?

- There are an estimated 1,770 child fatality victims per year due to maltreatment in the U.S., and average of 34 children per week.
- More than 80% of children killed were 0-4 years old.

What happens to former foster children?

- Approximately 408,425 children were in the foster care system
- 27,854 of those children aged out of foster care.
- Percentage of the general population that have a bachelor's degree: 27.5%
- Percentage of former foster children that have a bachelor's degree: 3%
- Percentage of the general population in jail or prison: 1%
- Percentage of former foster children in jail or prison after aging out:
  Males: 44.6%   Females: 16.4%
- Percentage of the general population who experience homelessness over the course of a year: 1%
- Percentage of former foster children who experience homelessness after aging out of the system: 24.3%
- Percentage of former foster children who report being unemployed 1 year after aging out: 47%
- Percentage of former foster children who reported living on food stamps 2-3 years after aging out: 45.4%

(First Star, 2012)

Creating New Statistics

IT IS primarily through the story of Derek Clark's personal experiences of being rejected by his biological family and growing up in foster care that we will begin to recognize and address the responses and resistance to adversity, past and present, that are displayed by youth in care. The utilization of a Response-Based approach to the experience of family separations and foster care experiences is intended to provide an alternative view to a systemic perception of deviance, pathology, and defiance. A review of grief and loss literature suggests that family separation, regardless of the justification(s), creates an experience of loss that is under-acknowledged in terms of positive social responses within the system of foster care. Grief can become complicated and confused when it is layered upon the existing ambivalent feelings from previous traumatic experiences, neglect or abandonment. Further to this, we know that the ways in which children and youth respond to and resist these experiences of adversity often receives a pathologizing social response from involved professionals, many times creating further harm. Some examples of harmful social responses may be assessing, diagnosing, and medicating kids for 'behaviors' that could otherwise be understood as responses to loss, grief, and/or trauma. This book is limited to the joining of ideas from the lived experience of Derek Clark as well as other former youth in care, and the combination of foster parenting and clinical experience of Shelly Bonnah. Beyond our own experiences, we draw from the richness of understanding that we have been invited to witness by youth and colleagues who join together in solidarity with the goal of creating change. Further research will be required to produce scientific evidence that supports this work.

Chapter One: Through the Eyes of a Child

"They said I had attachment Disorder. Really, I had a life disorder. I attached accordingly."

(Sarah, National Youth in Care Network, 2009)

[Derek] HERE I was, a child desperate for love and affection, a scared little boy who was getting ready for what would be the longest ride of my life. I can't say I remember the drive to the orphanage, or the place where kids were stored, but I do remember not bringing along any toys. I remember the sun being out and the sky being blue. The day was pleasant, warm, and peaceful, in stark contrast to the foreboding anxieties that were raging inside me. I didn't know where I was being taken, only that this day would likely be the darkest of my life so far. The longest ride of my life eventually ended at a place I considered an orphanage. It was a big building with lots of space and rooms. I figured it was an orphanage because all I saw were homeless and unloved kids. Kids who were no longer wanted by their Moms and Dads. I could see the sadness and fear in their eyes, and imagined that same fear must be showing in mine. We were now disposable, kids who could be thrown away or tossed overboard. Kids who were never to be loved or comforted by our parents again.

Who would have cared if we were drowned or burned to death? At this point, it was already like we were being buried alive. We were being killed, suffocated, by lack of love. We were

1

now the county's worry, pain and nightmare. My parents were weak in my mind, and now I had to somehow become strong and survive. I felt deep misgivings and anxiety, the memories were killing me. I kept thinking, 'Where is my big sister?' I thought that surely she would come and rescue me because she loved me. I expected her to show up at any minute. But nobody came. Here I was, a helpless little five year-old boy, and my heart no longer beat for anybody but myself. Hope was lost for me at that point. My little life as a boy who nobody could or would love began.

At this time, I wasn't even able to love this little boy. Plagued with insecurities and doubts about my self-worth, I was now going to have to make a home here in hell. I was left alone with all the bigger boys, who just stared at me like wolves salivating at their thoughts of feasting on a weak, vulnerable little lamb. I was the proverbial sheep being lead to the slaughter.

I was very alert and very scared. Very, very, very scared. There was no love here. This was a place of pain and ghosts. We were throwaways or misfits. Possibly we were angels who nobody recognized as such, but that could hardly have occurred to us at the time. This was to be my new home while a new family was being prepared for me. I didn't know who or what kind of people might invite me to share in their life. Or for that matter, if anybody would want me at all.

I remember thinking that my Mom would of course be coming back for me. I trusted that my mother's love would override whatever other concerns she had. I felt a deep hatred for my stepfather. He had taken my Mom away from me. If she didn't come back, I placed the blame squarely on his shoulders. I cried from loneliness and fear.

The older boys were antagonizing and threatening me, trying to push my limits. I got angry and taunted them back, so one of the boys pulled out a toothbrush with the end sharpened for use as a weapon. I ran for my life. I thought I was going to die. I knew what death was even at a young age. According to the county reports I had a kind of morbid fascination with death. Later that night, when it got dark, I grew even more frightened.

We slept in what appeared to me like a giant classroom with a bunch of beds placed in it. It was some kind of enormous warehouse for storing kids. I remember hearing lots of crying in the middle of the night, puncturing the silence. Other kids were missing their Moms and Dads, brother and sisters. Where were mine? I wondered why my brother and sister got to stay with our mother and I was stuck here in this sad, terrible place. Why was I rejected and deleted from the family? Was I special somehow, or was I just a piece of garbage? Why couldn't I just be a normal kid like others? A kid who had a family? Why didn't anyone love me? Why couldn't I just be a kid?

I still remember very vividly one of the most horrific abuse incidents which ever happened to me. It is so embedded in my soul that it feels as if it just happened yesterday.

It was a sunny day in California. The year was 1975. I was a kindergartner. I was a curious and tough five year-old boy. My mother, stepfather, half- brother, half-sister and I lived in a two-story townhouse. There was nice green grass in the front of the house. When you walked inside, you saw the dining room and kitchen on the right and the family room on the left. In front of you was a staircase with a black iron banister leading to the bathroom and the bedrooms. The bathroom was located at the top of the stairs. The house was furnished and I remember the wood being very dark with big lamps made out of clear orange textured glass. On the table and kitchen counter there would always be empty yellow Coors beer cans. I remember seeing lots of yellow Coors beer cans in those days.

I would often be outside playing in the tunnels under the main road overpass near our house. As a kid I called them tunnels but as an adult looking back, they were big storm drainpipes that went under the street. I am amazed that my Mom would let me wander and play over there at such a young age. I would love to hang out there and throw rocks at the metal siding of the pipes. When the rocks would hit, it would make a cool high-pitched noise that would echo through the tunnels. It would be exciting to sit under the overpass and hear the cars go honking by overhead. Sometimes I would find dead rats in there and lots of interesting junk. At times, adults would walk through, using the tunnels as a shortcut. Older kids would sometimes hang out in them. If I was alone, the tunnels would scare me a little, but I was tough and showed no fear.

One day, it was starting to get dark and I decided to head home. When I entered the townhouse, my mother and I started arguing. I also remember a few yellow Coors beer cans. My mother asked me to do something. I defied her and said, "Screw you!" but really using the F-word. This wasn't the first time I had said these words to my mother. In fact the F-word was one of my favorite words at that age. But this time when I said it, my mother snapped, apparently having had enough of my disrespectful language. With anger in her eyes, she grabbed my arm and tried to pull me up the stairs. I resisted and fought back. I was yelling and she was yelling. It was very chaotic.

I threw up a big struggle that got out of control, still she overpowered me, and I could not pull away from her. She pulled me up the stairs to the bathroom and physically forced me to the sink. While holding me there, she turned on the hot water full blast, running it until the steam was rising profusely. She kept yelling at me, screaming that I was never to use the F-word again, telling me how bad a kid I was. She emphasized how terrible a kid I was over and over again. I remember her yelling at me uncontrollably. I think she must have totally snapped.

What she did next was incomprehensible. She restrained my body and forced my tiny left hand under the scalding hot water.

I was screaming, out of control and trying to pull my hand

4

out of the water. It hurt so much as she held it there. I screamed "Mommy stop, Mommy stop!" I was crying so loud, it hurt so much. I could not believe my own mother was doing this to me. It was like my life was flashing before my eyes and my whole body was shutting down. It was like she never heard me. I then yelled "Mommy, you're hurting me, it hurts mommy, let me go, I love you." I tried to get away but she looked at me with intense anger and said I was a bad kid. I thought I could get away, that I was stronger than her. But I couldn't. I was only five years old. I was helpless and completely at her mercy. The skin on the back of my left hand was burned off. I have had this scar ever since, on my body, in my heart, and in my mind.

All the other physical abuse I could deal with, but this particular incident altered me physically and mentally forever. This was the final ticker for the time bomb that was about to go off. I was no longer an innocent little boy. I was now overcome with a sense of shame and anger that would last for years. I realized I was no longer good enough and that I was not really loved. I felt worthless and unwanted.

I wrote the following poem when I was a senior in high school, soon after my foster brother and biological sister were killed. I was continuing to be flooded with doubts about being loved, and questioned my own ability to make the choices that would secure me a better life. The poem is a collection of the recurring thoughts that I was able to turn into art. It helped me to have an expressive outlet for them, so that I could then analyze them and see if they were making any sense, and whether or not they exposed certain negative or destructive tendencies. And if so, whether my artistic expression revealed a way to overcome them.

Waiting nine months, waiting for their bundle of joy,
then from the time after birth,
the mother and father are in fear of what they created.

A second child to an alcoholic family,
his name is Derek Clark,
completely innocent, not knowing of his future calamity.

Well the boy started to grow,
And soon learned to talk,
The parents weren't excited about his achievements,
They would rather go for a walk.
Left him in the house with his older sister,
Seeing the Coor's beer cans
Never see his parents hit her.

Why would they hit him,
Why such abuse,
He was only one to four years old,
Not believing he had much use.

He once told his mom the F word,
She took him upstairs
To the bathroom and turned on the hot water
And held his hand under there.
With the hot water burning the skin off his left hand,
He was screaming for Mom,
But she didn't understand.

Leaving scars for life,
That will add to his nightmare,
Someday will affect his future,
If he doesn't learn to care.

They took all their anger,
Used him like a whipping boy,
Hit things against his head,
Threw him down the stairs like a toy.

When the boy was five,
The parents said he was out of control,
Off to Snedigar Cottage,
Where his life would begin to take its toll.
Staying there, he felt all alone
Then he got transferred to a foster home.

No need to feel all alone,
All he ever wanted
Was to be back home.

Alcohol was the source
Of this young boys detrimental childhood,
Never will he do the same to his kids,
Pain was something he understood.

So as a teenager,
The nightmare is still there,
Sweating the fear in his sleep,
Living the little boy's nightmare.

With scars to look at
And recalls of the past
This boy is making his own life
One about which he will be
Pleased at last.

The following is a paper I found in my journal from my teenage years as a foster kid. It was written in a moment of time that reflected my true feelings; although my behavior most of the time did not. I could not have known throughout those dark days and nights in the orphanage that I would ever be wanted; that I would ever be loved again. I wrote about my experience living on a farm with lots of animals. I love animals and the spirit of healing they bring to us. Animals are so in tune to the human spirit. As a foster child, they helped me learn how to love again when I felt no one loved me. Horses are amazing animals with feelings that can sense our sadness. As animals, they have special unique abilities to teach by example, how to love unconditionally, and heal the spirit of a wounded child.

As I lay in my hammock swinging in a grove of eucalyptus trees, the clean, fresh, sinus-cleaning scent sifts through my nose and I am able to reminisce about some of my greatest memories. They are still so vivid, and will be forever. Who can ever forget the combined smell of corn husks, pine and eucalyptus trees, beautiful flowers and roses set off against the sounds and odors of our farm animals? The sweet aroma of the beautiful flowers and the roses, which attract honeybees, drowns out the smell of horse and goat manure used as fertilizer for the plants. On the other hand, the manure attracts the flies. What a small price to pay for the setting of beautiful memories!

I remember the early mornings. I would have to wake up, go into the horse pasture, and help my dad shovel horse manure into the pickup truck. That was easy compared to going into the goat pen and carrying out loaded buckets and garbage cans full of goat

manure. The main problem was that the pen was not a flat piece
of land, it was at a tilt. So it was a little harder to carry the buckets out. Sometimes my parents would pay me twenty-five cents for each bucket I filled. Getting paid was nice, but I also enjoyed the fruits of my labor when eating fresh apples, zucchini, corn, string beans, cantaloupes, squash, broccoli and tomatoes.

"There's nothing like biting into a fresh cob of corn and having the kernels pop as you chomp down. Then there were the good old family picnics where we would all saddle up our horses and ride to Garin Ranch and partake of hamburgers, hotdogs, Jell-O, and cookies.

"My foster Mom would usually drive the car to the park and meet us there in order to have the hamburgers ready when we rode in starving for food. The ride was about two hours and the horses were grateful for the break as we ate.

At home I was responsible for training one of our ponies. His name was Bootie, an American white pony, very large and ready to take anybody for the wild ride of their life.

I calmed him down after getting bucked off several times. It takes a lot of courage for a young boy to get back on a pony after being bucked off. Now he is a fast, smooth and well-disciplined ride.

In the early morning I would get up and milk the goats. We had five that were milking and they would give about two-and-a-half gallons total. After milking, I would come into the house and filter the milk, put the date on the bottle and refrigerate it. Any effort was worth some fresh goat milk. I loved having a fresh glass of goat milk with chocolate chip cookies.

I come from a foster family of seven kids and sometimes there would be a few extra foster children. I think my mother and father's door is always open for a lost kid who needs good, loving parents. The atmosphere when I walk into my house is cheerful, with the helping hand of Mom and Dad.

Materially, the furniture is beat down, the carpet has been trod on over a million and a half times. The kitchen table is large enough for an army. There are toys lying around for people to walk on and break. It is not as clean as other people's houses, but what can you expect when you come from a large family who rides horseback, takes care of farm animals, plays in acres of dirt, goes dirt-bike riding, builds massive forts, climbs trees, and takes apart greasy motor parts. After all this we come into the house and sit down. One just can't have classy, expensive stuff when they live like that.

I wouldn't give up this place for anything, because we as a family have made this house our home, full of love and closeness. Special family ties have been made that will never be broken. There are too many memories to recall on paper, but I can say one thing: a home like this makes the grouchiest people smile because it's a true fairyland.

[Shelly] Derek is not alone and nor, unfortunately, is his story of loneliness and vulnerability an isolated one. Countless children and youth have stories of abandonment, fear, and shame of moving through the system feeling vulnerable and alone. The following brief stories are windows into the hearts of kids from Canada to the United States, ranging in age from 3-18 years old:

I remember the van. It was green and it belonged to the 'after hours' social worker. When it pulled into the driveway, it meant that someone was leaving and they usually didn't come back...I always wondered when it was going to be me. To this day I hate green vans...(Joe, 18)

Please. I don't want to go. I'll be a good boy. I'll use my potty. Please. I don't want to go. What are you doing with my toys? I'll be a good boy. I'll use my potty. Please...PUT DOWN MY TOYS...that's special to me...please...I'll be good...don't make me go...(Noah, 3)

A lot of the food was locked away in the foster parents bedroom... especially the good stuff. So once I tried to sneak in there to get some of it, and they had the door trapped with water on top of it so that I would get soaking wet. Now it says on my file that I stole from my foster parents...I didn't want to steal anything...I just wanted the candy! (Sabrina, 15)

Dinnertime in a new foster home is the worst. I do everything possible to avoid it. Families are so different about how they eat dinner. Some families all have certain places they sit every night and they freak out if I accidentally sit in someone's "spot". Then there's the 'manner's' thing. What can I use my hands for or do I always have to use a knife and fork, what about talking with food in my mouth? Do I have to take some of everything and if I do, do I have to eat everything on my plate? And the food itself...it's really hard to get used to other people's way of cooking and the type of food they eat...and they all think it's so normal. Finally...the awkward moment of how to leave the table. Do I have to wait for everyone to be done? Do I thank someone for the meal? What's her name again? Or am I supposed to stick around and help clean up, even though this isn't my house...but they keep saying it is my house now...but we all know the truth...(Candace, age 17)

I was on my way to a foster home after my dad beat me up...the first time I've ever gone to a foster home. First I had to wait in the Ministry office for over an hour because they couldn't find a social worker to drive me there. Then they finally found this guy...someone different than the one that I had already been talking to. I felt so uncomfortable because I would have rather had a woman social worker. He didn't say a word to me the whole way there...he just had this weird look on his face like he was mad or something. As we were pulling into the driveway he finally talked to me. He said, "Let's make this quick, I don't have time for this today". I felt like throwing up. (Angela, age 16)

Fostering isn't something every person is able to do. You often sacrifice parts of your own life for someone else's, along with the hurt of letting go. It creates a different definition of what a family is. You don't have to be related to be a part of a family. Over eighteen teens and children have lived with us over the years, and almost all of them make an effort to spend holidays and have visits with us. Growing up in a fostering environment has created the person I am today. My family opened our home to kids who needed love and safety, and in return we have bonds and have received love and loyalty that will last forever. Many people comment on how hard it must be without realizing the benefits of forming relationships that are meaningful and mutual. In the end we have been able to provide 'belonging to a family' for kids who came to us without knowing what belonging is supposed to feel like. (Shea, 18)

Through the Eyes of a Child
Instant Message

1. **Understand the context of external events in the lives of the children and youth coming into the foster care system.**

   - What have they experienced in their lives before the system became involved?
   - What do they think, feel, pray for, and fear?
   - What is their private logic? Why do they do what they do, and in what ways does it make sense to them?
   - Create room to speak the unspoken...using the children/youth as a guide for timing of these conversations.

2. **Acknowledge that grief and loss is inherently part of the experience of being a child in the system.**

   - Loss of family, belonging, community, familiarity, bedrooms, peers, belongings, IDENTITY...
   - Grief takes many forms, and the easiest way to express it for many children is through behavior.
   - Grief, loss and traumatic experiences are easily mistaken for behavioral disorders and treated as such.

EXERCISE

Close your eyes and try to imagine having everything that you know taken away from you. Try to imagine expressing the feelings that you have as:

a) A toddler

b) A primary aged child

c) A pre-teen

d) An adolescent

Chapter Two: Through the Eyes of An Adult

> Saying that everyone is welcome requires that we
> create spaces of inclusion and engage with the
> complexities of enacting respect. We structure safety in
> public and committed ways in collaboration with each
> other, and develop accountability practices that hold
> us to this ethic of belonging. We cannot work without
> these engaged practices that provide the scaffolding for
> an ethic of belonging.
> (Richardson & Reynolds, 2012, p.11).

[Shelly] MY PERSONAL experience of profound loss as a foster parent within the system of has provided the motivation necessary for me to become part of the search for a compelling alternative to current practices. As a foster parent to teenagers for many years, our family experienced all of the adjustments including the anxious moments; joys, sorrows, and gratification that I'm sure are shared with many caregivers across Canada and the United States. We have had the honor of watching them learn to drive, go on dates and graduate. We have had the heartbreak of letting go too soon or hanging on too long. Our biological kids were initially in their preschool years when we became a foster family, and we did our best to protect them from all that was developmentally inappropriate for them; we continually worried that our best was not enough. They heard language and saw conflict as young children that they wouldn't have witnessed otherwise while at the same time gaining brothers and sisters who will likely be a part of their lives forever.

The limited research into experiences of foster parents' natural children showed that foster children do have an impact on natural children. Foster children encourage positive experiences (e.g., sharing, responsibility, caring and independence), but these are coupled with experiences of loss (e.g., sharing the attention of parents), resentment and a wish to escape
(Bromfield & Osborn, 2007)

As our biological children approached adolescence and our youngest foster son was moving out, we made the decision that we would no longer be a 'practicing' foster family. We gave our official notice. And then the phone call came: "Would we be able to care for an eighteen-month old baby? Just for the weekend?"

That weekend turned into a year and a half, and during that time we had formed a mutual love relationship. We were inexperienced foster parents for children of his age, and had absolutely no heart armor—no self-protection. We were well aware intellectually that he was not our biological child and that it was unlikely that we would be in a position to adopt him, but emotionally we were inadequately prepared for what would happen when he left. The decision that he would go, or where he would be placed, was not ours to make. I wrestled with the deepest grief of my life; lightened only temporarily when I was able to see him for short visits. His first visible response to our brief reunions was to immediately take off his shirt and extend his arms to be lifted into a hug. I averted my face so he wouldn't see the tears. I understood this delicate request for connection as his way of seeking closeness without barriers—a universal human desire. In the months following our separation, his initial anguish gave way to aggression indicating a desperate attempt to grasp something beyond his reach and far from his ability to understand. I didn't understand either. That's what grief can do; it can flatten us.

A pivotal moment occurred when I was reprimanded at a meeting concerning him for being "unprofessional" in my grief; I was crying. After all, foster parents should understand that kids "come and go". My experience has taught me that what they come with is not necessarily what they go with; their relationships, their belongings, their dignity and their self-respect are all at risk of being left behind in the wake of circumstances and decisions that are beyond their control. I became overwhelmed both by grief and a need to protect my personal and professional dignity. I remained quiet throughout the remainder of a meeting where professionals described a boy who I'd come to think of as my own as sitting in a corner at daycare, crying and pulling out his own hair. His behavior toward others had become "aggressive" and there was speculation that he was developing early symptoms of "conduct disorder". He had just turned 3 years old.

The following story, written by a former youth in care, demonstrates the desperate longing that can induce specific behavior.

> *There was a great big guy who worked at the group home I was in when I was 14 years old. He was always really fussy about his stuff and liked to keep everything organized and neat. He was so big, that when kids got out of control, he would just walk up behind them and restrain them in a hold—kind of like a big bear hug. I used to grab his stuff on purpose and then run like hell...I knew he'd get mad and come after me. I used to do that on purpose. It felt so good to be held.*
> *(Shane Dobratz, 28, Former Youth In Care)*

As adult caregivers, guardians and supporters of children and youth in care, we are responsible for every detail of how they move through the system, when moving is deemed necessary. This is inclusive of the conversations with them and about them, and the information that we decide is going to follow them. For example, it remains disturbingly common for children and youth to transfer between foster homes with their belongings in garbage bags; the dignity of packing with consideration and thought removed as an option replaced with the urgency and immediacy of green garbage bags—a staple of every household. The underlying message, intended or not, is that these kids are dispensable and disposable like daily trash. There is no mechanism to ensure that the crucial components of their lives remain intact as they journey through the foster care system. As they use the most effective tool that they have, *their behavior*, to resist such systemic assaults, we often further assault them by responding with assessment, diagnosis and medication.

The 'end' of the system at the age of 19 is often a final, and severe, assault of relational abandonment and a series of fear inducing circumstances. Endless reports from youth who have left the foster care system confirm the devastating feeling of being "dropped" into a world that they are inadequately prepared for, without a support system. Unlike many other young adults, youth from foster care often lack 'family privilege' (Seita, 2005), the invisible privileges that come with the unquestioned knowledge that you will have somewhere to go on holidays, that you can move home if you lose your job, and that you can call if you are feeling lonely. This transition is commonly referred to as "aging-out". We contest that youth do not 'age-out' at 19 years old. *The system 'times-them-out', and they continue to 'age-on'.* To suggest that youth 'age-out' implies that their support ends as a result of *their age*; something innately unavoidable. To be accurate, the responsibility for this loss of support belongs to the system that has ***timed-them-out***.

The Linguistic Devices of Labeling, Minimizing & Hopelessness

YEARS AFTER leaving the foster system, Derek Clark was able to access his youth file through the California County and piece together the professional assessments, concerns and even some of the conversations that were centered around planning for him. These accounts are not random or haphazard: rather they involve the consistent use of the specific linguistic devices that:

a) Label,
- Language that directly or indirectly attaches the problem to the person.

b) Minimize,
- Language that minimizes harm to children and youth, or minimizes their value, worth and/or importance.

c) Communicate an Attitude of Hopelessness.
- Language that communicates adult hopelessness.

Derek ranged between the ages of 6 and 7 years old at the time of this documentation. The linguistic devices of labeling, minimizing and hopelessness will be underlined throughout the text. The following information was captured 'through the eyes of an adult' viewing the life of Derek Clark.

October 1st

Neural Test results: Neural grossly intact, normal for a four year old with IQ compatible for a four year old. Doctor feels there is mild retardation rather than something psycho-serial. He could perform skills but not up to age level. Not hyper-active, EEG Normal.

The psychiatric evaluation conducted when Derek was 6 years old consisted of approximately 18 hours of interviews in preparation of a final report. It is neither random nor haphazard that the statement is made that a psychiatrist **feels there is mild retardation.** Acting responsibly to this information, the adults around him responded accordingly at that time in his life.

November 12

Placed calls to eight different foster homes.

None interested at this time.

The linguistic device of hopelessness is evident within this brief file notation; making it difficult to imagine hope within the context of those eight phone calls. Eleven days after the psychiatrist sharing his feeling that Derek may be "mildly retarded" and although he "performs skills", they are not what they should be—a social worker would be obligated to share this information with prospective foster parents. How do professionals hold on to hope, holding themselves and each other up in a system that can be profoundly sad and desperate? And yet, we suggest that is exactly what they find a way to do. Notations such as this may find their way into the hands of the kids they are written about. They time-out of the system and often, as Derek did, request their files. A common experience is to receive their 'file' in a cardboard box, and then they are left to read it alone.

November 14

Spoke to Foster Parents. Derek wishes he could see his Mother.

This expression of Derek's wishes minimizes the depth of his longing. Who is he expressing his desire to? What is their response? How are the circumstances of Derek's life being explained to him? How is he responding?

November 23

Test Results in. Doctor says at least average IQ. <u>Not dumb.</u> Shows severe emotional problems and is hyper-anxious. I discussed with foster parents that I am looking for another placement and advised them to start preparing Derek. <u>He messed pants</u> for ten days. Is fighting at school with younger kids. I placed call to new foster home. They would consider having Derek for a visit. Placed call to current foster mother to arrange visit. She says Derek wants to stay but accepts not being able to.

<u>Labeling</u> Derek 'not dumb' carries little distinction from labeling him 'dumb'. It is the language of deficit. In 1976, such descriptive terminology as 'messed pants' may have been commonplace throughout government files and foster parent reports. Dignity-stripping language is used to describe, report on, and 'treat' children and youth on a daily basis. This may not be intentional, but we have yet to raise our collective consciousness to a level that we no longer accept this way of talking about kids.

November 24th

Picked up Derek for a visit. We discussed family. Derek says he wants a bike, puzzles, a camera and toys. I will check with the mother.

Derek <u>seemed a little apprehensive about visit, but was not visibly upset when he met with new foster family</u> and the younger kids,

New foster home visit went well. He was delighted and told foster mother that he wanted to stay forever. Played with a pony, and was told about goats. He had a problem getting off mini motorcycle, but foster mother was firm and warm. She explained there were rules. New possible foster family feels Derek is a smart child, is aware of things around him. The placement has been okayed.

Derek is 6 years, 3 months old. Derek's background includes "extreme physical and economic impoverishment during infancy, and a father who brutalized the boy and his mother during the same period" (Report of Psychodiagnostic Evaluation: See Appendix 1). His mother and stepfather also physically, mentally, and emotionally abused him. After spending time in a county facility, Derek had been in an emergency foster home for 4 months. By the age of 6 years old, he had learned the art of focusing his attention on external objects, distraction, and maintaining a demeanor that drew little to no attention (when that was his goal). Until this point in Derek's life, the social responses to him were predictably negative—his parents had rejected him, his sister had abandoned him, school had expelled him, doctors had labeled him, peers had ostracized him, foster families had shuffled him, and bullies had bullied him. It would be understandable, and prudent for Derek to approach his new foster family as if he wasn't 'visibly upset'.

Something very different happened in that visit. The social worker made note of it, and more importantly, Derek felt it. For the first time in his young life, someone recognized that Derek is smart, and they let him know that they saw it. He wanted to stay forever. Hope is injected into the notes of the social worker at this point.

December 3rd

Talked to Derek's mother. She says she wants to see him. Mother gets teary when thinking about the new placement. We discussed long term plans. She still wants him to return at some point, and isn't in favor of an adoption. Says she is willing to participate in therapy but husband won't. Husband says it is Derek's problem, not his. We discussed the need for changes before Derek should return home. She said she doesn't know if she wants to go through with them. Things are fine with Derek. He does have emotional problems and is sometimes anxious. Derek was fond of his last foster home but makes it known he is going to be with new foster parents forever. Derek asked about Mom.

The above entry appears to reflect an accurate account of a conversation with Derek's mother, free of labels, minimizing or hopelessness. It also reflects the theme that will run throughout Derek's life in the foster care system: Derek asks about Mom.

December 20th

Derek is doing well. He wants his chalkboard and eraser. Derek is not slow. Does have problem with large motor coordination. He is clumsy, but small motor coordination skill ok.

Has bad toilet habits and defecates to get back at foster parents when he is mad. He admits it to be the case. He is a very controlling child, and needs to have control over what goes on around him. He can be a difficult child but the foster parents are enjoying him. They are able to deal with him and are interested in helping him with his problems. His Mother sent a Christmas card to the foster parents but not to Derek. Derek refers to his mother and stepfather by their first names now. He no longer calls them Mom or Dad.

Labeling: "not slow", "clumsy", "very controlling", and "difficult child"
Minimizing: "He can be a difficult child but the foster parents are enjoying him"

This entry recognized a pivotal transition in Derek's loyalties between his biological family and his foster family. It is interesting, in terms of timing, that Derek's resistance to not receiving a Christmas card may have been transitioning from 'Mom and Dad' to first names—perhaps his way of saying: "I'll fully reject you before you fully reject me".

January 7th

Mother, Stepfather, and brother visited and were happy to see Derek. Foster parents say Derek is having school problems. Sees the problem as not being able to cope with kids. He is not ready to be in school if he can't compete with kids. He uses his strength to bully kids and also teachers. He seems to be doing better with control, and has more problems with neighbor kids than home. The foster parents are concentrating more on his weak points. That should change. There reactions to small things were too strong as well. They need to ease up on that. They feel Derek is growing up and changing too. Foster father feels his role to Derek is as a father, and did some discipline. But the discipline is mainly responsibility of foster mother while he is working. Mother would like to take him home for a visit. We discussed therapy for biological mother and stepfather.

Hopelessness: "He is not ready to be in school if he can't compete with kids.

Labeling: He uses his strength to bully kids and also teachers.

Hopelessness: The foster parents are concentrating more on his weak points.

Minimizing: Unhealthily identifies with strong people like the Six Million Dollar man.

Minimizing: He thinks he has a bionic arm.

Labeling: Recommends a special class for severely emotionally disturbed children

Derek calls stepfather by his first name, no longer calling him Dad.

Although Derek didn't ever get to see his biological family face-to-face or hear their voices after the age of 6 years old, information was delivered to him through sporadic letters from his biological mother, and one letter from his biological sister. Those letters will be part of Chapter 3: Disable the Label.

Through the Eyes of a Adult
Instant Message

1. Youth do not 'age-out' at 19 years old. *The system 'times-them-out', and they 'age-on'.*

2. The linguistic devices of labeling, minimizing and hopelessness are used throughout professional verbal and written discourse pertaining to children and youth in care:

   a. **Labeling,**
      - Language that directly or indirectly attaches the problem to the person

   b. **Minimizing**
      - Language that minimizes harm to children and youth, or minimizes their value, worth and/or importance.

   c. **Communicate an Attitude of Hopelessness.**
      - Language that communicates adult hopelessness

EXERCISE

Think of a time that you have felt labeled. How have you responded, and how have others responded to you? What did you do?

Chapter Three:
Disable the Label

> I am here today because people like you never gave up on people like me.
>
> (Derek Clark)

[Derek] AT THE age of 6, I found myself in the foreign world of the foster care system, and for the first time in my life I didn't know who I was or where I belonged.

I feel like a reject.

I had been totally kicked out...dismissed.

I was thrown away.

Why would any parent give up on his or her own child?

They gave up on me and the most painful truth is that they kept my brother and sister. I was considered the 'bad kid' and the good kids got to stay with mom and dad. At this time in the foster care system, I was completely lost physically, emotionally, mentally, and spiritually. As a child who was feeling lost and hopeless, I was 'on guard' and full of anxiety, anger.

My walls were completely up.

I did not trust anyone.

I did not love anyone.

I had learned to rely on myself.

here Do I Belong?

Interview Between Shelly Bonnah & Derek Clark

December 23, 2011

Shelly: You were in a stable foster home with people who loved you, and your biological family gave you the gift, as I've heard you say, of not pulling you in and out of their lives for years. And yet...you didn't really settle. Even as a young adolescent, you were still running away and talking about 'going home'. Can you speak to that?

The reason I'm asking is that I think that after several years of loving a child and trying to recreate a sense of family, many foster families 'give up' when they feel rejected by kids who don't seem to be connecting or their behavior may be interpreted as an indication that what the family is doing is not enough. I think you may have something to say about this.

Derek: I believe the reason I never really settled was the memories and the knowledge that I already had a mom, brother and sister. There is that force within that pulls you to your biological family for some reason...knowing that you don't belong in this foster home and that you already have a family. My foster brothers and sisters had their biological mom and dad and I felt that I deserved one too...and I knew I had one!

I really don't believe that my foster mom and dad could have done any more to bring more love into my life. It was the fact that I knew I was a foster kid. If I had been adopted as a baby with no recollection of a biological mom and dad, I probably would have trusted and loved much more in my life. But if I was adopted as a baby and then my adoptive parents told me at age 5 that I was adopted, I probably would have had self-doubts

28

and wondered why I wasn't good enough for my own mom and dad. Why was I given up? Adoptive parents could say, "you are special" and "we chose you", etc. but the fact of the matter is that when you are rejected, you feel lost. I have met many kids who were adopted as a young child or a baby and still had the longing to bond with their biological parents. It is an undeniable force.

Shelly: So you had these incredible foster parents. They turned out to be incredible in your eyes. But I wonder if—when you were 12, 13, 14…did you know, beyond a shadow of a doubt, that if you continued to make decisions that would test everyone around you…violent decisions…that you wouldn't have to leave there?

Derek: No, I thought that I would be going. There were times that I ran away and times that I wanted to substitute my friends' parents for my foster parents. It even states in my county records that I wanted to leave this foster home. I wasn't thinking right back then. I would blame my foster parents for not letting me go back to live with my mom. That was really misplaced anger, when in reality, it was my own mother that was stopping me from coming back. She was not interested in reunification or therapy for her issues.

Shelly: So *you* wanted to go…but did you ever wonder if *they* would want you to go?

Derek: There were times. It states in my county records that they thought it might be time for Derek to leave. Lets face it, my foster parents had 7 other children and I was the one who was bringing a lot of tension and turmoil to the family dynamics. I don't believe that they wanted me to go. I believe that they thought that I was going to have better behavior as time went on. But I was there for years and my behavior, violence and lack of respect for adults and authority continued getting out of control. Let me tell you...they are saints because even when their patience was at an all time low, they still found enough love inside to keep giving and giving. They never gave up! I believe their strength came from God to deal with me because their strength and perseverance all comes back to my mom seeing me in that vision 2 weeks before she even met me or knew who I was. She believed that 'if I let Derek down, I let God down'. Because she saw me in a vision that she believed was from God. So, she was like "I can't get rid of him. I can't".

But there were times, when I was shoving them around, throwing rocks at my dad, threatening them over and over again...

Shelly: Threatening them how...what did you say?

Derek: I called her a bitch and every other foul name in the book. I threatened to hurt them, stab them and destroyed many of the walls in their house. At 15 or 16 years old, I was at a church campout and the pastor was telling me what to do because I was acting up. I walked over to the pastor, threatened him, pushed him, and was going to punch him. The next thing that happened was we were down on the ground and he was trying to restrain me. I had no fear of God or a pastor and here we are getting into a real fight, the pastor of a church and me. Man, I was crazy back then. On another occasion, I even went to the ground with the Boy Scout Leader. There were many other times that I threatened adult figures. I really didn't have any respect for adults, which I am sure stemmed from not respecting my own mom and dad. If my own mother and father could literally give up on me, how could I trust another adult? I felt that all adults were going to let me down so I became their nightmare. I didn't have any respect for my mom and dad—I didn't have respect for any adults. I didn't have respect for anybody. That's the reality.

Shelly: How did your parents respond when you were doing those things—pushing them around and threatening them? What did they say? What did they do?

Derek: I had to work. I lived on a farm. They came up with the saying, "if you are going to shovel out crap to people well then you are going to shovel crap". So every time I got in trouble, my temper was escalating out of control, or I was being disrespectful, I would have to shovel poop. I know a lot about chicken manure, horse manure and goat manure. They would start off at one bucket (5 gallon bucket) and if I didn't stop at one bucket of manure, they would give me another bucket. At one point in my rage, I got up to 25 buckets of manure. What I would have to do is take a shovel and fill each bucket with the poop and take it up to the garden and put it around my dad's plants. He considered the manure "feeding the soil".

Shelly: And you did it? You'd call her a bitch…and then they'd tell you to go to work…and you would just nicely go off and do it?

Derek: Oh no! I'd throw a big temper tantrum. Some big conflict thing. But in the end, I needed to eat a warm dinner. I did not like eating a cold dinner.

Who Am I?

[Derek] WHEN I was 15 years old, I was really out of control with my anger and disrespect to my foster parents. I had just been suspended from high school for fighting and my foster parents were frustrated and probably extremely discouraged. I had really been thinking about my biological sister at that point in my life and wondering where she was and what she might be doing. She would have been 25 years old at that time. My foster mom called the county to tell them I was in trouble again at school and my social worker came. I sat in his car as he attempted to 'set my attitude straight' and magically get me to be a better person. I yelled back at him *"you don't know me"* and he replied: "I want to know you". He reached behind my seat, opened up an ice cooler to pull out a soda, and then offered it to me. I decided to make a bid to him: I told him that I want to live with my older sister. I really wanted to get out of this foster home or run away. I felt that I did not belong there any more and it was time to go. I didn't trust the social worker but I thought that I could use him to my advantage and try to get my sister's address from him or find another home.

He surprised me. Within a few weeks, I got my sister's address. I wrote her a quick letter with excitement, stating that I hoped she remembered who I was and that I remember her being the one who gave me love as a young kid and how she would protect me. I let her know that I wanted to see her and could not wait for her reply to my letter. I did finally receive a letter back from her. It took quite a while for her to write me. I am sure she was shocked to receive a letter from me as I had been out of her life for 10 years. It is still confusing that she never once wrote me a letter in those 10 years or ever tried to get in touch with me. I was reaching out to her and to my mom and yet they never reached out to me. It is an awful feeling but yet, I had hope that they would connect to me and be available to me. Right until the end, they never were. For me, it was a childhood filled with disappointment because I longed for a connection to my "real" family.

The following letter is the reply that my sister sent to me when I was 15 years old. This would be the only letter, the last letter that I would ever receive from her. I still have this original letter. I quickly replied to this letter and even sent her my phone number. I had so much hope that we were going to be together again...brother and sister. I waited for a letter or a call for months. I would pray that she would respond, yet nothing. Unfortunately the following letter is the only one that I ever received from my sister while in the foster care system. I was continually let down every day when I did not get a letter in the mail. Every day I had hopes that would be crushed by the end of the day and yet, I would hope again that tomorrow would be the day. Almost a year went by until I received a letter from my biological mom stating that she was sorry for waiting months to tell me but that my sister was shot and killed on mother's day several months back. I was shocked and unable to comprehend or process that kind of bad news. How do you grieve for someone you have loved your whole life but never really known, and can barely remember? Once again, removing the option of going to her funeral from me highlighted my lack of belonging to that family. Her death was a loss and another profound rejection of me. I was left alone and in the dark—again. I wondered if they were ashamed of me, because if I had gone to that funeral I would have finally met my biological mom, brother and all the extended family. I had been thrown away and hidden so that she didn't have to think about me...but I thought about them every single day of my life. I kept thinking one day, they will want me back...but that day never ever came. I was a sore in my biological mom's eyes and a complete reminder of the mistake she felt she made and shame she carried. I have often wondered what would be different in my life now if I had attended my sister's funeral back then. I was 32 years old when I discovered that I had 5 aunts and uncles and cousins. I felt like I was the hidden kid and that my mom was so ashamed of me. Aunts and Uncles would tell me that they had no idea where I was and that my mom really didn't talk about me and they didn't want to bring my name up with her because it would make her feel bad. Isn't that crazy, I have 5 aunts and uncles? I was definitely erased from my family and it was great to finally become visible and meet every one of them.

Here is the last connection that I have to my sister:

Jan. 4, 86

Dear Derek,

Received your letter a while ago. I was real surprised to hear from you. Sorry its taken so long to answer you. I've been kind of busy with Christmas and all. How was your Christmas? What did you get? I heard you wanted an electric guitar. Well, did you ever get one?

Thank you for your picture. I have a very good looking brother! I can't believe you're 15 already! Sounds like you had an interesting summer. You like a lot of outdoor sports. I want to try parasailing. Didn't you try that? I just found your letter and I thought you had tried that.

What did you do over your Christmas vacation? I was thinking of coming up there to visit my friend Sue. She lives in Hayward too. I don't know if you can remember her. You were pretty little then. If I do I'd like to stop by and visit you okay?

How are things going for you? Fine I hope. What grade are you in at school? Do you like it? There's so many questions to ask? Well for myself I'm 25 now I can't believe it myself. I can remember when I was your age. I got married when I was 19 yrs. I have 2 children a boy his name Tyler and my daughter is Chelsea. They're very close in age. Tyler's almost 6 yrs. Chelsea just turned 5yrs. I've been living in Escondido since I got married which will be 6 years. Its okay but I'm tired of it. I'd like to move. I don't work. Just been home taking care of the kids. Tyler goes to Kindergarten now. So now I'm going to find one. I might go to school take some night classes.

Are you interested in girls yet? Boy, you're going to be tired of all these questions. Remember you have to answer them all. Give me your phone # so I can call you.

I really miss you. Please don't ever lose contact with me. I wish I lived closer to you. If I don't make it up there, I hope that one day you'll come see me. I'll send you a picture of me in my next letter. I have some film to develop.

I'm going to close for now. Write back sooner than I did.

Take care

Cuz I care

Love your sister

[Shelly]   Whether placed in foster care by family agreement or through government removal, the transition experience from a family of origin to a foster family is a neglected subject in the published research that is easily available to professionals working with children and youth. Typically, the troubling behaviors of children and youth in care are described in common discourse as *effects*: "negative end-states...slotted into pre-existing, culturally-based, deficit frameworks developed in psychiatry (DSM), psychology, social work..."(Wade, 2005). A causal explanation describes behaviors of youth in care as "caused" by early childhood trauma, attachment disorders or the fostering system itself. Frequently, their responses to the adverse circumstances in their lives are (mis)interpreted through the lens of psychological pathology, inviting professional interventions that focus almost exclusively upon behavioral management.

When a kid goes into care, they're angry. They miss their families, their whole routine is screwed, everyone automatically thinks the kid has something wrong with them because of how they act... (Research Participant, Lambe, 2006).

Throughout this book, we are highlighting Derek Clark's troubled and troubling childhood behavior as understandable responses to the circumstances of his life. These circumstances included traumatic incidents and profound loss before and during government care. Moss & Moss (1973) identify that a child's response to family separations is parallel to death and bereavement, although minimal research exists outside of the aboriginal culture regarding the unique experience of loss when government care is introduced. It is, however, increasingly recognized within attachment literature that a primary sense of belonging is essential before anything else matters (Brokenleg, 2008). Belonging is commonly absent for many children and youth in the system; they are yearning to be known, for their lives to be witnessed, to feel healthy touch.

Social workers; I always wondered what their role with me was as a youth in care. My social worker was always all dressed up and always smiled at me. I saw him from time to time depending on how much trouble I could get in. Why was he around? What did he do exactly? I suppose he took care of all the paperwork I caused, or perhaps an extra set of eyes on me every few moths. I always wondered why they were called "social" workers when you almost never had the chance to be sociable with them. They were rarely there to be social with.

Shane Dobratz, 28, Former Youth in Care

Despite having an optimal foster family, by Derek's description, he struggled both internally and behaviorally to discover where he authentically belonged.

Where Do I Belong?

Interview Between Shelly Bonnah & Derek Clark

December 23, 2011

Shelly: You developed some behaviors as a child that were cause for a lot of concern...they were 'diagnosable' kind of behaviors. But when we look at all of the events in your life, kind of one by one...and we recognize the loss and the trauma... those same behaviors actually start to make quite a bit of sense. So, for example, when we talk about your memory of that day when your mom dropped you off at Snedigar Cottage...do you remember much about that drive?

Derek: What I remember is the lack of conversation. The void. She took me to this place that I didn't know and it was the first time I'd really been taken anywhere that was outside my home or the school or the lake. I remember being alone with my mom and being dropped off. That was it. No 'I love you' or 'I'll miss you' or 'you're going to get help, Derek' or 'I'll be back for you' or anything like that. Well...she proved that she wasn't coming back for me...it was kinda like you drop a dog off at the shelter or pound. You're tired of the dog—you can't stand the dog and thankfully there's a shelter where you can drop it off or you're going to drop it off on the side of the road, right? You just have that strong desire to get rid of it no matter the cost, well that is what my mom and stepdad did.

And so...this was the human shelter and these were the kids who weren't wanted, I guess.

I kept thinking though that my sister would come get me. My sister was 15 at that point and I was 5. She was the one who always gave me love and it felt like she protected me from the abuse, but no one came back for me.

Shelly: At that time…You were only 5 years old…but did you realize what that place was?

Derek: No, not really, but I knew that people were mean. I knew about prisons from TV and I felt like the 'new fish' on the block. The new kid; I didn't know anybody, and I was scared. The lamb in a lion's den. I remember this one kid sharpening his toothbrush so it was a weapon. You can take the plastic and rub it on the concrete and keep flipping it over until it gets sharp. These kids would be tough during the day but at night, when the lights went out, these kids would be crying wanting their mom and dad…

Shelly: In the first day…week…you were frantically putting all of this information together about what has just happened to your life, and you're 5 years old…

Derek: I don't remember my mom saying "I'm dropping you off for good" or "I'm never coming back for you". But I remember the look on her face. This was awkward for her. She and my stepdad had enough of me, this adorable little 5-year-old kid and now was giving away her own flesh and blood.

Shelly: Do you remember the time, at some point later, when it crossed your mind in a definitive way 'She's not coming back'?

Derek: Yes. It was in my foster home. From the shelter I went to a foster home and then went back to the shelter and then the court ordered me to go back home. I went back home for a few weeks and then my stepdad and my mom finally dropped me off for good. I went to another foster home and she visited me once, and that was the last time she ever visited me. I didn't know for months or maybe even a year later that my mom would not be visiting me anymore….they just never called and never came back.

Shelly: And nobody ever said to you "This is over with him or her?"

Derek: I don't ever remember.

Shelly: So it was kind of left up to you to figure that out—-just over time?

Derek: Yes…I just had to process it. Now I would get a letter maybe once a year or something…maybe Christmas or my birthday from my mom…or maybe a letter here or there during the year. But the last time I saw her was when I was 6 years old and then the next time I saw her, I was 30. The last time I heard her voice I was 6 and the next time I heard her voice I was 30. I never had a phone call…never saw my brother again…my sister…poof...everyone just disappeared…even when I was a teenager…even when I was an 18 year old…a 22 year old…a 28 year old…nothing.

Shelly: And when you were 30, you initiated the contact?

Derek: Yes, and what I found out was that my mom feared for herself. She thought I'd come back and take revenge on her. She went through 3 very abusive husbands and I was a reminder of a very abusive husband that raped her and abused her. I actually don't know if she ever married my biological dad, I don't think so. He was very violent and physically abusive and would rape her. I remind her of him—I'm sure that's part of the reason they got rid of me. I was a violent little kid—she was scared of me. When I met my biological mom in my 30's that was one of the questions I had for her. "Why did she stay with my dad?" and she stated that he was so good looking and was scared to leave him. I have never had the feeling to ever want to find him and establish a father/son relationship. As far as I am concerned, it was a blessing that he gave up on me and never tried to make contact with me. My mom changed my last name to Clark in an effort to make sure that he would not find me because he wanted to kill me.

Shelly: So somewhere along the way, you process this and realize they're gone and your life now is with your foster family? What did you do…what was going through your mind?

Derek: I remember sending letters asking when can I see you again? You haven't visited me in a while. When can I see my brother and my sister? But I don't remember those letters being answered.

Shelly: How often were you sending those letters?

Derek: I would probably send a letter a few times a year. And I think the big thing, when I was a bit older, like 11 or 12, was that I wanted to know who I was. What were my nationalities? Who am I? Why did you give me up? But I never got answers. Then I noticed the relationship between mother and son changed again when she stopped signing 'mom' and started using her first name instead. That happened at a young age… maybe 8…she just stopped signing 'Love Mom'. It wouldn't be love mom anymore. It would be Love Mary. I remember thinking, "who is Mary?"…That's my mom. I believe she was letting me go fully by not signing mom anymore on her letters and cards. I was really baffled by that. In my teenage years, she would then start signing "mom". But to be honest that 'mom thing' was not real to me anymore. Although I had this desire or longing to want to be back with my mom, her actions said everything...I mean everything! I had been in the foster care system for so long by then and I was tired of hoping that she would come back for me, so I just acted out in more rage and violence and then I would write to her about it. She would respond and say, "Try to be good Derek" and then I would ignore her. So I fed her bits and pieces of my crazy teenage life which didn't bring us any closer but probably scared her even more that I was coming back for her to take revenge... like a movie. That probably explains why we waited so long to meet each other as adults. I was 30. The fact of the matter is that we could have met when I turned 18 or 22 or 27 and so on, but she would not reach out to me. I had now turned into an adult and I know that she was scared. I have since been to her house and seen her fear of others and fear that my biological dad was going to come back and take revenge on her as well. Even now, she lives a life of fear. My biological dad died back in 2007 or so, so he is not coming back and what a shame that he never got his life together and missed out on so much. I am nothing like my dad or my mom. I have broken the cycle.

Shelly: Can we back up a bit? When you realized that transition happened, that she had stopped referring to herself as mom, what was going through your mind? What were you thinking about that?

Derek: I was literally thinking I didn't have a mom anymore. It was an awful and hopeless feeling. It was bad enough knowing that she had given up on me, yet was staying in touch by letter every once in a while, but now not signing the letter as mom, it was just plain awful. Some parents are so selfish with their own emotions that they really mess up their kid's heads. Aw, thanks mom for now totally shutting me out of your life and turning me into the invisible son? Ashamed of me like I am a monster?

I was just a reminder of her mistake and she needed a way out! It wasn't long after that that I started calling my foster mom 'mom'.

Shelly: Oh…that's when you made the switch…your foster parents became 'Mom and Dad' to you.

Derek: I believe so…because I realized that not only by her actions of never visiting me and now signing the letter by her name was the final clincher when I knew that she had given up on me. She was done with me.

Shelly: Do you remember talking to your foster parents about any of that?

Derek: I don't remember but most likely not as I was not the type of person to open up and share my feelings. I merely acted them out with anger and clowning around but to talk to me and have me expose my inner feelings...no way!

Shelly: But in a way…you did reveal your inner feelings. You gifted your foster parents with the title 'mom and dad' at that point of your life. You made a choice there…a clear one. Maybe that choice revealed grief and love at the same time? You may not have had a conversation about it, but your choice revealed your feelings.

[Derek] The following letter was received from my biological mom once I was an adult, responding to many of the questions that I had been asking her throughout my life.

Dear Derek,

I don't know how to start this letter. Guess I'll answer your questions first. I've answered some of these before.

Didn't you ever get my letters? First of all, how dare you ask me if I am a recovering alcoholic. I'll have you know that I'm a damn pretty nice woman everybody likes. I never was an alcoholic. How dare you (ha ha), not mad, just feel bad cause you think that! What made you think that? Did the foster parents tell you that? Your step dad is an alcoholic. I have tried hard to make him quit but he won't he's hooked on it. So all I can do is pray…I went through hell years ago. My married life wasn't easy nor was my childhood. My dad was an alcoholic. He was very strict with us. Very! So I married at 17. I had a very sad life when I was young growing up.

No love in my home. My mother was a very good lady. Never drank or smoked. Very nice but she stayed with my dad til the end. She suffered a lot but stuck by him for years. He was mean to her. My poor dad even though he was awful with us, we all cry for him and love him. I guess he lived a very sad life. We were very mistreated when we were all young…you don't know me, I wish you did, you would love me…You must think I am an alcoholic mean crazy woman. Well I am the opposite of all your thinking of. I'm well liked and respected by all of my friends. I am a lot of fun. I am a fun loving person. I'm very easy to get along with. So I don't know why you shouldn't get along with me. Ya, you are right, you are right, you don't know me. It's very sad cause you don't. Maybe someday you will, if it is your will…

About your dad? Don't ask to much about about him cause we all don't know. All I know is that he is in his late 70's, still gets around, lives from 1 state to the next. Last time I heard, he was very handsome. Sang a lot of country songs, very good voice. Sang nice, but always in trouble. Always! I didn't know much about him when we first met. He wouldn't tell me much but he was always in trouble. He wanted to marry me but I couldn't. He drank a lot of wine. He used to mistreat me and hit me a lot. He abused me a lot. I was afraid of him. So I left him when he was in jail for bookmaking that I didn't even know of. I was pregnant with you. Corlaine (your sister) and I lived in a little apartment not far from the job where I was waitressing. I worked hard all day to make ends meet. I had to support your sister and I. I wasn't getting any child support from your sister's dad. He never sent me money. So I worked hard to raise her the best I could. She was 71/2 when I left her dad. He was another crazy one. He was a truck driver and never home. He loved women. Your sister and I were always alone while he was out painting the town. I didn't need that so I left him. Oh Derek, I could write a big full book about my life. It was your sister an I and my little Derek in my tummy. I didn't have the money to get a baby sitter, so after school, she'd sit in the restaurant for hours a day. I used to cry a lot cause I worked hard and just to see her sit there in the booth everyday playing the jukebox and doing homework. It just tore at my heart. But what could I do? I had no income but what I worked…hardly nothing. I made ok tips but not a whole lot. I didn't even have a car. This old 70 year old man came in sometimes to eat. He felt sorry for me. I think he thought I was nice! He used to watch me walk a lot with your sister so he gave me his old car. It left gray smoke behind when I'd drive it around. But at least it was a car. I didn't make enough for furniture so I'd shop at Goodwill for a bed and a few clothes. I didn't even have enough to buy you a stroller. I did save money to buy you a bed. It was hard cause again your dad didn't support me either. So here I was back in the frying pan. My life was no better, now worse. Hard.

Your cousins found you a stroller around the trash dump. I was happy to get it. I cleaned it up...

I hadn't seen your dad in a while and I was at the hospital giving birth to you. Your dad came to see you and me at the hospital. I didn't want him to cause I was done with him, He always knocked the hell out of me and I was afraid to call the cops. He'd beat me more. So I made a break, thank God to get away from him when he was picked up by the cops for bookmaking with horses. He was in jail a long time...I never married your dad, if I did, he would have killed me or hurt me bad. So I didn't thanks to God.

Your Mom

[Shelly] A framework has evolved from the cumulative efforts of many people applying Response-Based ideas to working for youth in care. This framework will be outlined in Chapter 4, and has been designed to elicit a positive social response from professionals while also understanding youth behavior within the context of both past and current individual experiences. An enhanced understanding of behaviors, both as professionals and youth in care can contribute to the development of non-pathologizing interventions that assist youth in making meaning of their experiences while gaining a sense of control and responsibility in their lives.

Disable the Label
Instant Message

1. Understand the Context of Behaviors

- Troubled and troubling behavior is often an understandable response to the circumstances of a child or youth's life.

  This does not replace taking responsibility for violent behavior, at any age.

- Understand the potential for family separation to be parallel to death and bereavement

2. A primary sense of belonging is essential before anything else matters.

EXERCISE

Imagine your sacred places of belonging, and the people who belong there with you. Now imagine a powerful stranger insisting that your places, and your people, are no longer safe for you.

a) What is going through your mind?
b) What would you say to that stranger?
c) What would you do?

Chapter Four: Some Response-Based Ideas

> When youth feel a sense of injustice: they will resist.
> When youth feel powerless in decisions that affect their
> lives: they will resist.
> When youth feel that their safety & dignity are
> threatened: they will resist.

[Shelly] WHEN CHILDREN and youth enter a system of professional care, they become dependent upon that system for justice, decision-making in their lives, and the protection of their safety and dignity. In many cases, these are the very things that they have required protection from, and the reasons for introducing foster care into their lives. The Response-Based approach provides a framework to understand how children and youth respond to, and resist, the circumstances of transitioning into care and the often-frequent moves that occur once they are in the system. Resistance is ever-present in the face of oppression, violence, and situations of adversity when a person's dignity is at stake. While we recognize that these are not the experiences of all youth in care, the statistics suggest that there is systemic violence occurring within the system itself. It is frequently against the will of kids that they are being moved, medicated, separated, and dropped at the age of 19. Resistance may not be effective in stopping or even minimizing situations of injustice, feelings of powerlessness, or dignity-stripping circumstances. It is, however, ever-present and universal in the preservation of safety and dignity.

Observable 'behavior' is one form resistance and is viewed under this approach as understandable and healthy when considered in the context of responses and resistance to unhealthy circumstances. The nature of social responses received by children and youth in care are paramount to their 'survival' in the system. Simply stated, this means that the ways in which professionals surrounding youth respond to, talk about, and diagnose kids is commonly more significant than the trauma(s) they have experienced: this is how we explain the difference between kids who 'successfully' survive the system, and kids who linger in their struggles.

Clinically, the Model of Sustainable Wellness (MSW) (Bonnah, 2008) provides a guide for professionals to respectfully enter a conversation about the unique experiences and understandable responses of children and youth in care. This information is unlikely to be gleaned through the referral forms, assessments or the words of others. In fact, a Response-Based approach requires professionals to assume that a child or youth is the primary expert in contributing knowledge to what he or she needs. We gain that knowledge through an understanding of their words, their behavior, their interests and their resistance, as demonstrated in the following example. This account of living in a group home setting will provide examples of a young person's responses and resistance to such unique circumstances, which are underlined:

This group home was the perfect place to <u>cause trouble</u>. Kids were released from jail to here and foster kids that had a <u>bad reputation</u> and no home to take them in were sent here. I <u>made many friends</u> here, because there is <u>some sort of ally tie</u> when you live in one of these places. The sad thing is that friends you were really close to could be there in the morning and gone when you got back at night, with no way of knowing where they went. <u>It felt like mini jail.</u> All the food was locked up and there were no rides. Staff changed every few hours and they had their staff room, which was locked also. If we wanted to get *into our rooms they would have to unlock it for us. They could search our stuff whenever they wanted. There were always kids in and out. I pushed the limits here at this group home. Throughout the years, I was off and on in this home. My longest stay here was 9 months, which was at this time. One of the boys really touched my heart. He was lonely because he didn't have parents and he had no one. He fascinated me because he told me that he broke into a family's house in the morning and didn't take a thing, but just sat there wishing for what he did not have; a family...*

I remember someone putting gum in between all the forks and spoons. I hated eating here.

Staff had these books in which they would write all this stuff about us to tell our social workers, probation officers, or the cops. Curiosity is a strong motivating force for me. One day I took the book out of the office and ran and locked myself in the bathroom to read it. Staff called the cops and I was arrested, if you can believe that...

Katherine McParland, 23 (Former Youth In Care)

Formulating responses as resistance requires the practitioner to listen deeply to the language used by the youth, and to match their language and verbal style as closely as possible (Wade & Adams, 2006). Using specific examples, such as "When you cause trouble and push the limits, is that your way of testing people...finding out something important that you need to know? It sounds like your secret way of forming ally ties?", or "Have there been other times in your life when curiosity has really paid off for you?" The language of responses and resistance challenges the dominant discourse of symptoms, pathology and pharmacological treatment. The diagnostic approach minimizes personal responsibility by creating a "reason" outside of the individual to explain both personal and social responses. These explanations may include depression, anxiety, conduct disorder, attention deficit disorder, or oppositional-defiant disorder. Rather, understanding actions as intentional resistance to situations that are perceived as harmful or oppressive additionally serves to increase personal responsibility.

Central to this model is a core attitude demonstrated by professionals of hope, equality, acceptance and compassion, without which I would deem this way of working with children and youth to be ineffective. Although not yet scientifically proven, the young experts who have participated in a therapeutic conversation guided by the MSW appear to relax physically, actively engage in a mutually created dialogue and report thinking of themselves more positively and in a significantly different way than they have had in the past.

Best practices with youth in care are not always clear, universally accepted or easily implemented. Systemically, professionals encounter obstacles in the forms of legislation, mandates and insufficient support. Additionally, there is an invitation to become indoctrinated into the accepted professional discourse of pathology, revealed through the common language that communicates pessimism/hopelessness, judgment/superiority, detachment/rejection and labeling/diagnosing. And yet, we gravitate into this field with something overwhelmingly in common: we universally seem to want to make a difference.

A Model for Sustainable Wellness (Bonnah, 2008)

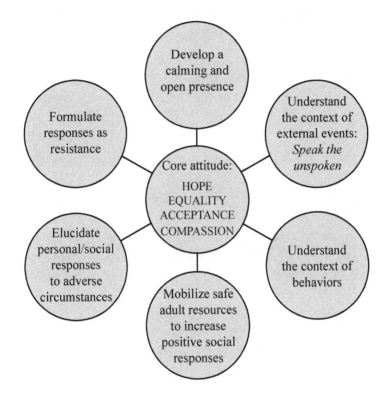

REGARDLESS OF the topic, there is clinical relevance to the practice of pausing and considering what we know as helpers in this field, how we "know" it and questioning this body of knowledge.

At times our work as community workers can replicate the kinds of dominance we hope to alleviate; accommodating people to lives of poverty, and participating in practices that can serve as social control. Some workers sign on to cynicism; throwing up their hands at institutions and bureaucracy instead of rolling up their sleeves and working to change policy; and maligning other workers and programs, like dogs under the table fighting over the bones. As an activist, all of these tactics were familiar to me, and disheartening. (Reynolds, 2010, p.2)

Adopting a position of not knowing defies the coveted "expert status" that lends us our credibility and oftentimes, our influence.

In the therapeutic enterprise we must tread a fine line between some, but not too much, objectivity; if we take the DSM diagnostic system too seriously, if we really believe we are truly carving at the joints of nature, then we may threaten the human, the spontaneous, the creative and uncertain nature of the therapeutic venture. Remember that the clinicians involved in formulating previous, now discarded, diagnostic systems were competent, proud, and just as confident as the current members of the DSM committees. Undoubtedly the time will come when the DSM-IV Chinese restaurant menu format will appear ludicrous to mental health professionals (Yalom, 2003, p. 5).

The statistics that represent youth in care who have been diagnosed, hospitalized for mental health explanations and placed on medication strongly indicate a dominant discourse and theoretical orientation of pathology. Yet there is an emerging body of research that suggests those with mental health diagnosis, given adequate social support yet otherwise devoid of "professional intervention" will achieve a level of wellness that no longer requires hospitalization or medication (Whitaker, 2002). The Medicine Wheel of Responses (Richardson, Wade, & Bonnah, 2012) demonstrates some common responses from youth in care physically, spiritually, emotionally and intellectually. The Model of Sustainable Wellness aims to provide professionals with a framework to learn about the responses and resistance of youth from each of these four quadrants.

THE MEDICINE WHEEL OF RESPONSES; YOUTH IN CARE

- Running Away
- Hiding
- Hitting
- Tensing up/going limp
- Saying "NO"

- Prayer
- Visualization
- Music
- Leaving the body
- Friendships

PHYSICAL

SPIRITUAL

EMOTIONAL

INTELLECTUAL

- Anger
- Sadness
- Self-medication
- 'I don't care' stance
- Sexual connection
- Cutting

- Strategizing for safety
- Scanning for opportunity
- Using private logic
- Humor
- Outwitting adults
- Planning

Acceptance & Trust

Interview Between Shelly Bonnah & Derek Clark

January 30, 2012

Shelly: I'm imagining you as a young person...not just in your foster home but also in the school system, with other kids, probably everywhere you went...just figuring out how do you trust a person—who is trustworthy? You probably had a way of figuring all of that out really quickly. Are you aware of having that skill?

Derek: That's a very interesting question, because to be honest with you, I don't trust very many people at all. I am very guarded about who I let in my inner circle. I have an instinct...I can look at people and feel a connection to their soul and it's instant for me. I can generally see if that person has qualities that are going to complement my life and add value. I need to know if it is worth the risk to expose some of my vulnerabilities and be able to trust them to be able to take the risk of them letting me down or breaking my trust. In reality, I really don't trust many people. I mean, to go through what I have been through in life...seriously, who would trust at all? Hey, at least I do trust and open up to trusting more but on my time and terms. As a teenager...it was the same as well. My walls were always up.

Part of the whole trust issue is that...I don't like exposing myself to the point where I'm going to be open to pain or the reminders of my past. I've already been hurt. Why go there again, unless it is there with a few special and trusting individuals? So,I don't trust very many people. Trust. I have a hard time trusting the pastor, the church leader, the Boy Scout leader. Not only for what I've been through but all the molestation and things you hear about people getting close to your family. I'm very apprehensive and study people. I have to protect my family and protect myself. I have to understand what peoples' agenda is and what their intentions are. I have to step back, watch and be intuitive because some people have an agenda and will show their true intentions.

I guess when people see me, the guy on the stage and they may like what I say—they still don't know me. They're seeing me at the end of the movie sharing all of my pain and carefully chosen vulnerabilities to expose. If they had been there with me through the beginning of the movie...the middle of the movie...maybe they wouldn't have liked me.

Shelly: So they're seeing what you're choosing to let them see. That makes sense...Isn't that what most of us do?

Derek: Exactly. All these doors opened for me in 2006. But before that, I had a pretty good-sized mortgage brokerage in California and I did well financially and socially. I would have never exposed myself like I expose myself now. Because I was all about money and I was all about success. No one knew I was a foster kid. Nothing was shared with my friends or with anybody—it was not something you shared. I did not want to open up my soul. Nobody got a peek inside of who I was. Nobody got a chance to peek inside and see who I really was. When I wrote "Goodnight Soldier" it started awakening my spirit. What I realized after starting to expose my past and vulnerabilities was that success wasn't about money but rather about significance and sharing hope with others. When you give others hope, it fills your hope void as well. Life is really about helping others and not living a selfish life but rather a selfless life.

Even though my foster parents have been with me for years, there is still a big rift between the biological kids and the foster kids in my family. Some of the biological kids don't like that my parents ever fostered. And I just think, well, if they have to choose between their biological kids and their foster kids, maybe, just maybe, they'll choose their biological kids. Although, they never ever gave up on me, I will always have that thought.

So there's that whole trust thing. I believe it is pretty normal for someone that has been rejected by their biological parents and had their hopes consistently let down. Even though I know that they love me…there's still that issue or insecurity that I was given up on and that…I'm not as good as a biological kid. In reality, I am good enough! But sometimes that little hopeless foster kid within still tries to be fed with the 'poor me' pity. I don't feed it; I would rather feed the powerful Derek, full of life and full of passion. I don't ever think that you can get rid of that little kid within that yearns to be fed; I just know how to be aware when he calls and ignore it. It gets easier and easier when you are aware of that, it has no power over you. I am not defined by my past, I am defined by what choices I make right now. I own my thoughts, actions and dreams.

Shelly: What do you mean by big 'rift' between the biological kids and the foster kids?

Derek: At times, we'll have separate Christmases, Thanksgivings, Easters, where they'll spend time with me, and then they'll spend time with their biological kids to keep the peace. Not that I'm second best, I don't feel that, but sometimes I feel I can't let my guard down all the way because…it's their biological kids…they're complaining "hey mom and dad, you guy's screwed up our lives because you brought foster kids into our home. Because of foster kids you brought sexuality and all the other crap."

So would they choose me over their biological kids? The answer would be no. These are their kids and I feel that I am one of their own, but the unknown is always there...because it happened to me already once with my own biological parents. I appreciate my foster parents so much and I'm grateful for what they've done for me.

[Shelly] The following account is a contribution from my son, with some of his views about growing up in a foster home:

My strongest memory as a foster family is my oldest brother joining us. I remember him as incredibly shy at first, but with time he became a part of our family and grew into becoming a brother to my sister and I. These types of relationships only developed a handful of times, but when they did it made even the most difficult of situations feel worth it. I've seen kids lose they're mind in anger over things I couldn't have understood at the time, but somehow our family always had a unique effect on them. Even kids who were incorrigible at first would eventually adjust to our family's way of life. The only negative point of view I have towards fostering are the flaws in the system, like losing our connection with a three-year-old baby who we loved. Our family will never be the same without him. Out in the world I have a brother who doesn't know who I am; we raised him in the most critical time of his emotional development and yet, now we wouldn't recognize each other in public. Aside from this, growing up as a member of a foster family has been valuable in many ways and an overall positive experience.

(Jon Ibsen, 20)

Shelly: Given your love and appreciation for them, and clearly their love for you—there's no way they would have done what they did if they didn't love you genuinely—what do you do with the doubt? I understand that you've learned how to keep it from taking over...

Derek: There's that little piece in you that has that little doubt, right? You know, I've already been through this once or twice. I couldn't trust them because they gave me up...so...if your own biological family will give you up, I think we're almost wired to think "why would you want me" or "are you going to give me up"?

As a helpless and hopeless kid that was relying on adults to give me shelter and food, of course I had many doubts. Doubts about if God even loved me, doubts that I would stay in one place for very long, doubts if I was going to make it out of the system alive. I was full of doubts sometimes and very suspicious of others and what were there intentions for me. At that time I had no faith in anyone or a God that truly loved me or looked out after me. So my way of dealing with all of my doubts was to put them on the back shelf of my mind and create more erratic hysteria through anger, violence and disrespect. It would literally take my mind off all my insecurities and doubts and put the focus on my strength and power—or what I thought was powerful at that time. Being a little kid full of anger and rage, it afforded me the sad opportunity to hurt others and by doing that it took away my own pain for that moment. I was able to inflict it on others and that became the focus instead of dealing with my own doubts and issues, I would simply pass my pain on to the world like some beast from another world. You have to realize as a little kid, I was sometimes withdrawn from reality and living in my own world and every now and then, this world would feed my inner world of pain. I loved to explode and deliver a powerful raging attack. It was a rush.

As an adult it's very different. I don't focus on it because if you feed it, you breathe life into it and it can turn out to be an ugly monster looking to destroy your life. It could take years to slay that beast. So many wasted years and lost opportunities to improve life because the time is spent on something that is stealing the joy and passion out of your life. So, I just move on and am very careful of what I breathe life into. I want continued success and peace in my life and so I feed my spirit with great things that are going to bring out my best. Sure, there are times when doubt will try to settle in and make a home in my spirit, but that doubt doesn't last too long in me. I never let myself be a victim!

Shelly: I think it's important to recognize that this 'doubt' probably exists to varying degrees for most kids in care, and some are able to manage, silence, control it as you are describing, and others may be more controlled by it, don't you think?

Derek: Yes, the doubt can cycle and spin in your head as a constant "why…why…why?" "Why me?" For me, that only happens for a moment, and I catch it as a crazy moment and say "what's up with that?" I may talk about it with my wife or think about it and then that's the end for me. For others it can suck the life out and take their power. I don't let anything take my power. If you have plenty of love and value in your life, then the pain of the past cannot overtake your world. It can if you allow some pain to get through and you start dwelling on it and then by doing that you feed it and fuel it and before you know you are encapsulated with pain. Pain can hold you captive for many years and steal all of your joy, enthusiasm and passion for life. I love that quote that states "You can't start the next chapter of your life if you keep re-reading the last one."

Shelly: So returning to my earlier question...at a young age, you were able to figure out who was trustworthy in a fairly effectively way...is that right?

Derek: Yes, I believe I have an ability to connect with people's spirits. I know how to ask questions, and when I meet people I scan them and analyze instantly.

Shelly: And when it comes to trust, you are extremely cautious with others, but it sounds like you deeply trust yourself...is this true?

Derek: Oh yes! I would not be where I am today in life without trusting my intuition and myself. I don't trust logic per se. I am very intuitive. If I was very logical and analytical, there is a good chance that I may have not gone through marriage because of my trust issues or even starting a business because I don't have the experience or a degree. So I totally follow my intuition...

Shelly: ...And you trust your intuition...?

Derek: I trust my intuition completely! I don't trust logic all the way. I trust what I believe, what I feel, and I go for it. All the things against me say that I shouldn't be where I am today. That's logic. That's what was fed to me. Those were the labels.

Logic says I should be a failure.
Logic says I should have spent time in jail.
Logic says I should be in a mental institution.
Logic says I should have killed somebody or taken revenge on my mom.
Logic says I should be mentally handicapped.
Logic says I should be a drug addict and alcoholic.

Logic says that I should not be a great parent,
Logic says that I will never bond with another person,
Logic says that I will never be happily married.
Logic says that I will never hold down a job.

But I don't believe the labels that logic can box us in with. I have a free mind and I don't have to agree with others' logic. I do it my way. I follow my intuition. I only trust myself.

Shelly: When you think back to when you were much younger, did you always have that kind of trust in yourself? When you were 8...9...10...years old? Do you remember trusting yourself to that degree?

Derek: I remember saying "I don't know how long I'm going to be in this home. I have to survive this. It's all about me." One of my big dreams at 8 or 9 years old was to be a rock star. I said, "one day I'm going to be a rock star and everybody's going to love me... " I'll never forget that.

The closest I ever got to being a rock star probably would be 'Goodnight Soldier' when it went everywhere...millions. And...I still had people *hate* me. I still had people send me letters...send letters to the editor of the newspaper hating my song, hating the meaning of the song. And I got threatening calls! When I met the President of the United States it turned it up a notch and it was all over the newspapers. I thought everyone would love my song and the meaning of it but I learned right then and there that I could not please everyone. Even though, I really wanted the world to like my songs and have them accept me, it was not going to happen. You cannot make everyone like you. It was definitely a lesson because in my mind as a little kid, I was going to grow up and thought that everyone was going to love my music and me. Many people do, but not everyone and I am fine with that now. It was not a realistic expectation.

Dreams, that's what I can trust in. I will always have my dreams and no one can take those from me. As a kid, I always thought that something good was going to happen for me in this life. Many people told me that...I was a mess-up, I was a buffoon, I was out-of-control, so a lot of people fed me "here he goes again acting crazy". But deep inside I believed I had something special. I always trusted I was a good person but that other people couldn't see ...who I was. It was almost like I felt I had to live up to this label..."Derek's out-of-control". I remember at 18 years old when I went through counseling and they said "we understand you have anger and rage issues" and I remember saying "no I don't...my anger is my power!" Growing up, I would try to inflict fear in others so that no one would mess with me. But I always trusted myself. Definitely.

Safe Adult Resources

SAFE ADULT resources are defined as adults who demonstrate support, or positive social responses, to children and youth in care. Within the social support literature, positive social responses are characterized as instrumental support, emotional support and information support (Ullman, 2000).

> *This foster mom is my favorite woman in the whole world. This lady gave me the courage to start changing my life and to separate myself from negative influences. This is the first time I was not treated differently than biological kids.*
>
> *Katherine McParland, Age 23 (Former Youth in Care)*

A comprehensive literature review regarding kids in care substantiates both my clinical and personal familiarity with the unrecognized victimization that occurs when a young person is in receipt of negative social responses.

> *One of the foster homes that I lived at was with a single parent of three kids. We used to go camping and she would stay up late drinking with her friends. The foster mom and her kids had a gorgeous trailer to sleep in. The foster kids would have to sleep in tents beside it. I hated it there because I didn't have the money her kids did for the concession or games, etc. I did a lot of reading and got very depressed.*
>
> *Katherine McParland, Age 23 (Former Youth in Care)*

The above provides a clear example of a young person responding, understandably, to her circumstances with sadness and isolation after receiving a negative social response from the adult charged with caring for her, and the other children surrounding her. It is not uncommon, and is equally problematic, to disregard the social responses that youth are receiving and diagnose their responses and/or resistance, which can easily meet diagnostic criteria.

Examples of negative social responses include:

a) "Taking control of *youth's* decisions (e.g., telling her what to do),

b) *Youth* blame,

c) Treating *youth* differently (e.g., stigmatizing responses such as pulling away from the *youth*),

d) Distraction (e.g., telling the *youth* to move on with her life), and

e) Egocentric behavior (e.g., responses where the support provider focused on his or her own needs instead of the *youth's*)

(Ullman, 2000, p.258)

**The word *victim* has been replaced with the word *youth.*

The intentional way of guiding a process that identifies meaningful connections and mobilizes safe adult resources is implemented to increase a young person's sense of hopefulness. Kids in care are typically denied family privilege (Seita, 2005), as they are moving through childhood and/or adolescence virtually unclaimed by adults. Meaningful connections to youth may be revealed as their relationship(s) to a teacher, coach, former foster parent, current foster parent, social worker(s), counselors or any adult member of their family of origin. The identification of these relationships serves to recognize where, and with whom, youth experience their sacred places of belonging. A Response-Based approach cannot be successfully adopted without a consistent and core attitude of hope, equality, acceptance and compassion. Bringing forth responses and resistance as active behavior(s), thoughts and emotions to sustain the integrity of autonomy allows for increased accountability. This acknowledges an individual's responses as intentional, useful and most often, healthy, if considered in the context of their life's circumstances.

RESPONSE-BASED QUESTIONS

How do you figure out who is trustworthy?

If you get that feeling like they're too "risky", what do you do?

How long have you trusted your intuition about people like this?

Do you think people have any idea that you're checking them out so throughly?

What goes through your mind?

How do they usually respond when they notice you back away?

"When I meet people, I scan them and analyze them instantly."

What are you feeling in these moments?

So you might take a few steps back: what else do you do?

What are you scanning for in that instant?

What's the difference if your intuition tells you this person is safe?

Do you have other private ways of protecting yourself like this?

How do you repsond to them? What do they do?

(Wade & Bonnah, 2012)

65

Some Response-Based Ideas
Instant Message

1. Central to this model is a core attitude demonstrated by professionals of hope, equality, acceptance and compassion, without which I would deem this model ineffective.

2. "Safe Adult Resources" are defined as adults who demonstrate support, or positive social responses, to children and youth in care.

3. Within the social support literature, positive social responses are characterized as instrumental support, emotional support and information support.

When youth have a sense of injustice: they will resist.

When they feel powerless in decisions that affect their lives: they will resist.

When youth feel that their dignity is threatened: they will resist.

EXERCISE

Think of a child/youth with a behavior or situation that you find challenging and develop 5 curious questions that communicate hope, equality, acceptance and compassion.

Chapter Five: An Assessment Lens

> Trauma and our responses to it cannot be understood
> outside the context of human relationships. Whether
> people have survived an earthquake or have seen
> repeatedly sexually abused, what matters most is how
> those experiences affect their relationships—to their
> loved ones, to themselves and to the world. The most
> traumatic aspects of all disasters involve the shattering
> of human connections. And this is especially true for
> children. Being harmed by the people who are supposed
> to love you, being abandoned by them, being robbed
> of the one-on-one relationships that allow you to feel
> safe and valued and to become humane—these are
> profoundly destructive experiences. Because humans are
> inescapable social beings, the worst catastrophes that can
> befall us inevitable involve relational loss.
>
> (Perry, B. & Szalavitz, M., 2006, p. 231)

[Shelly] A COMPREHENSIVE assessment of children and youth who are entering the foster care system is essential in determining an appropriate placement and adequate services, in order to create stabilization. This is a critical statement, because the 'lens' of the assessment is desperately important and has far-reaching implications. There is current acknowledgement for the need to respond to the high rate of 'mental health' issues presented by youth in care with comprehensive assessments that are widespread, as a way of early identification and intervention (Tarren-Sweeney, 2010). A recent report produced jointly by the Representative for Children and Youth and the Office of the Health Officer in British Columbia, Canada, highlights this urgent need for assessment:

This report again underscores all-too-familiar issues – lack of planning, inconsistent use of assessments, lack of focus, and inability to monitor. Better outcomes for children require a much higher degree of coordination, focus and accountability...

A year in the life of a child is a very long time. Each year that passes without essential yet basic improvements to our child-serving system means more B.C. youth veer off onto paths of unmet potential and troubling futures. Progress on recommendations made in our previous joint report on education outcomes has been very slow and inadequate given the magnitude of the problem.

Some youth enter care because of their involvement with the youth justice system, while others are already in care and then engage in criminal activity. Such distinctions do not alter the special relationship of trust and responsibility placed on the Province. This special relationship, of being 'the parent' entrusted with shaping the futures of these vulnerable youth, demands more careful assessments, so that plans of care reflect not only the past experiences of these children and youth, but their future potential. (Representative For Children and Youth & Office of the Provincial Health Officer, 2009)

As we have emphasized in previous chapters, there are a variety of ways to understand behaviors, thoughts and 'symptoms', some of which lead directly and swiftly toward a mental health diagnosis, and a particular type of social response from the professionals involved with the care of systems' kids. Statistics reveal that what follows is an unequivocally high rate of medicating the minds of youth. The risk is that a movement toward universally accepting a comprehensive mental health assessment will produce a generation of 'mentally ill' youth in care.

The assessment of traumatic incidents before and during government care is clearly absent from standardized practice for a variety of reasons. The child welfare system has a clear mandate to "care for and protect vulnerable children and youth" (Ministry of Children and Family Development, 2012).

The paramount tasks of this system—the substantiation of maltreatment and assessment of risk of future harm— frame and constrain practitioners' focus. Maltreatment substantiation primarily requires identification and documentation of observable, behaviorally based forensic evidence. Resources in child welfare agencies are often very limited, and practice that is considered extraneous to the primary mission may not be encouraged (Cameron, Elkins & Guterman, 2006, p. 58).

It may be unrealistic to hold the expectation that professionals bound to such a specific and principled mandate as child protection would additionally be either mandated or qualified to assess the complexity of circumstances that surround traumatic experiences, loss and grief. A multidisciplinary and highly collaborative approach is undisputed as 'best practice' for meeting the individualized needs of children. This practice is both of the highest quality and the lengthiest in duration. It is undoubtedly the latter that becomes prohibitive in the urgency of decisions that cannot wait for collective input. The Neurosequential Model of Therapeutics (Perry & Hambrick, 2008) provides one example of a "comprehensive approach to the child, family, and their broader community" (p. 39) in terms of assessment of both neurodevelopment and trauma. This approach to assessment will fail to serve in emergency circumstances, but rather by design is deliberate and individualized to ensure the incorporation of history, current reality(s), and possibilities.

A primary challenge of the neurosequential model is the need to integrate a fundamental understanding of neurodevelopment and early childhood into the existing working models used by the different professionals collaborating in the interdisciplinary team. The range of educational background, personal history, and experience among these professionals can complicate the process of creating an integrated, developmentally sensitive set of interventions. The most effective way we have found to address this is to provide cross-disciplinary training activities that are "case-based." (Perry, B, 2006, p. 49).

While the need for thorough assessment is widely acknowledged in order to create stabilization and the evidence-based model(s) exist for individualized, collaborative assessments to be implemented, numerous barriers continue to prevent the organization of such a fundamental shift in practice. Namely, as emphasized by the Pew Commission on Children in Foster Care (2004) and by the Committee on Integrating the Science of Early Childhood Development (2000) in *From Neurons to Neighborhoods*—child welfare services and mental health services require a much stronger level of collaboration than they have reached to date (Benoit, 2006). This is a difficult yet not impossible partnership; it requires a blending of mandates, philosophical approaches, and shared resources.

A comprehensive assessment must include a full analysis of how children have responded to, and resisted the circumstances of abuse, violence and oppression in their lives. This is markedly different information than knowing his or her history, which is the common language found within virtually every comprehensive assessment process. Whereas the collection of historical data tends to be on a macro-level, a Response-Based conversation is a series of micro interactions that include the circumstantial details of what has occurred, how children and youth respond to and/or resist the circumstances in their lives, and then how they have been responded to in return. The information revealed through the interactions of responses and resistance will often create a clear picture of an individual's private logic and mental wellness versus mental illness. Finally, it is imperative, as part of the assessment process to understand the nature of social responses received by children and youth in care. The research is clear (Ullman, 2010) on the role that social responses play in the recovery from traumatic incidents, and yet this information is blatantly absent from traditional assessment questioning to date.

If authentic collaboration between child welfare services and mental health services is achieved, a third and arguably the most crucial partner, the caregiver, is required for accurate assessment and stabilization of children and youth in care. The third partner has been frequently minimized, silenced or omitted from the therapeutic assessment.

> Children with relational stability and multiple positive, healthy adults invested in their lives improve; children with multiple transitions, chaotic and unpredictable family relationships, and relational poverty do not improve even when provided with the best "evidence-based" therapies. (Perry & Hambrick, 2008, p. 43).

Caregiver's could, and should, be central members of a collaborative team of professionals working for kids in care. Although it may be current practice to include caregivers, their training, education, confidence and credibility within the larger team of professionals does not necessarily grant them equal standing or contribution. Just as Child Welfare workers and Mental Health workers often work independently, so do caregivers, only to a much greater degree. This is a fundamental problem. Foster parents have what seems to be unimportant information when viewed as isolated incidents; yet threaded together these details tell a story. Caregivers have a chance to understand the 'private logic' of children and youth; why kids do what they do in a way that is explainable and understandable. Without the private logic these actions and behaviors may appear pathological. Foster parents have historical details that are left out of reports because they weren't 'significant' enough, they have current realities that emerge unexpectedly as magical stories which describe the adults whom these young people are becoming and these stories hold their dreams for a future of hope and destiny. None of these things are revealed as genuinely during an assessment or in a therapy room. And yet, the intimate details of where children and youth have been, where they are, and where they want to go will provide the opportunity to both accurately assess them, and plan for the stability of long-term placement that takes fully into account who they are—as individuals. This is crucially important information.

The "freezing" response that the body makes when stressed—sudden immobility, like a deer caught in the headlights—is also often misinterpreted as defiant refusal by teachers because, when it occurs, the child literally cannot respond to commands. While not all ADD, hyperactivity and oppositional-defiant disorder are trauma-related, it is likely that the symptoms that lead to these diagnoses are trauma-related more often than anyone has begun to suspect.

(Bruce Perry, 2006, p 51)

[Shelly]   As the severity of a youth's negative behavior increases, so does the likelihood of a diagnosis (Sherperis, Renfro-Michel & Doggett, 2003). Increasingly, young children are being diagnosed with bipolar disorder, a mood problem marked by symptoms of depression, invulnerability, minimal fatigue, increase in activities, a marked increase in sexual behavior and high risk-taking behavior (Elliott & Kelly, 2006). This is only one of numerous diagnostic labels used to describe behavior that challenges the caregivers of children and youth in foster care. Research indicates a significantly higher rate of prescribing psychotropic drugs to children in the United States as opposed to other developed countries, therefore indicating a correlation between the "quick fix" culture and a medical approach to "fixing" challenging childhood behaviors (Elliott & Kelly, 2006). The drugs, sometimes major tranquilizers, act by numbing brain cells to surges of dopamine, a chemical that has been linked to euphoria and psychotic delusions (Harris, Carey & Roberts, 2007). This approach masks the grief and trauma associated with family separations and other forms of adversity.

Responses to adverse circumstances are frequently diagnosed as pathological behaviors and the cycle of separation and rejection becomes increasingly prevalent. Research has demonstrated that "when children behaved in avoidant ways, foster parents tended to respond as if children did not need them; when children behaved in resistant ways, foster parents tended to respond angrily" (Dozier, 2005, p. 27). Dozier highlights the limitations of the foster care system by calling it temporary, by its nature, and lacking in long-term foster parent commitment to the children placed in their care (2005). Dr. Francine Cournos recognizes that one of the greatest paradoxes in working with children who have experienced profound loss is that despite their deep need for connection and compassion; they often push people away (2002). Behavioral specialists are frequently employed to provide support and interventions, including behavior modification, cognitive interventions and appropriate developmental functioning models (Sherperis et al., 2003), while doctors oversee the prescribing of medications. A medical diagnosis of an attention disorder, disruptive behavior disorder, affective disorder, and/or anxiety disorder is typically followed by a pharmacological treatment (Elliot & Kelly, 2006). Despite the ever-increasing trend of diagnosing and medicating children and youth in care, there remains no definitive test for attention or disruptive behavior disorders (p. 59). Consider that there is wide recognition around the goal of foster home stabilization, yet some children may be placed in up to 50 or 60 homes (Child Welfare League of Canada, 2003, Lambe, 2009) as a result of the difficulties presented by their behavior. In the absence of acknowledging challenging behaviors as their responses to the adversity faced in their lives, there is an overwhelmingly prevalent diagnostic approach taken in attempt to minimize the challenges and silence the resistance that is frequently communicated through behavior. This has become a medically legitimized way of responding to behavior, often against the will of young people, with highly adverse consequences in many cases.

Foundation and Application of Response-Based Interventions

Response-based counseling does not replace collective efforts to address violence or other social problems but affirms individuals' despairing and hopeful responses as eminently practical forms of social action and expressions of human dignity (Wade, 2007, p. 16).

A RESPONSE-BASED model of therapy (Coates & Wade,

2007), where opportunity is created to view problematic behaviors as understandable responses to the context of one's life, is highly applicable to youth in care. This approach challenges the dominant discourse that suggests deficits, often irreversible, within a child's personality, attachment ability and social functioning. A Response-Based practice is invested in identifying resistance through the "uncovering of contextual details, eliciting responses to adverse events, and formulating behaviors as understandable responses given the circumstances" (Wade & Adams, p. 3).

Any mental or behavioral act through which a person attempts to expose, withstand, repel, stop, prevent, abstain from, strive against, impede, refuse to comply with, or oppose any form of violence or oppression (including any type of disrespect), or the conditions that make such acts possible, may be understood as a form of resistance. (Wade, 1997, p. 25).

The following excerpt from an interview with Derek Clark (2011) provides an example of uncovering contextual details in a discussion around his anger, violence and trust. The behaviors consistent with resisting harmful or oppressive circumstances in the lives of youth in care can sometimes be harmful or oppressive to others. The explanations of cause and effect, such as "she was sexually abused" or "he has attachment disorder" minimize the youth's personal responsibility. "Responsibility for the abuse may be attributed to external events and stresses, the actions of others or medical/psychological conditions, over which the perpetrator feels he has little influence or control" (Jenkins, 1990, p.13). Resistance that takes the form of violence is intentional and youth can, and should, be held fully responsible for their acts of violence (Stefanakis, 2000). Formulating responses as resistance does not negate accountability in favor of compassionate understanding.

Rather, it requires the listener to consider the entire truth; the victim *and* the perpetrator or the oppressed *and* the oppressor. Compassion is generated from the relational bond that respects the struggles of the youth as important and maintains distance between actions and identities.

As a young boy who then entered the foster care system, I had a fascination with knives. I would always fantasize about cutting and hurting people with a knife. From the 'normal person's' point of view, I was a pretty twisted little boy. When I was about nine years old I found a razor blade, and started to carry it around in my pocket. One day when my neighborhood friend, about three years younger than I, would not do what I said, I took out my razor blade and threatened him. I wanted him to go down a hill on his Big-Wheel. With the razor blade held out threateningly, I told him that if he didn't go down the hill on his Big-Wheel, I'd cut him.

He wouldn't go down the hill because he was scared to. He was about 6 years old, and it was a big hill. As I was yelling and swiping the air in front of him with the razor blade, he became very frightened. Trying to protect himself, he stretched his hands out to shield his face, and I proceeded to purposely cut his hand with the blade. It cut through the webbing of skin between his thumb and first finger. The cut went completely down to the bone. Blood was flowing everywhere. He ran screaming all the way home. I then went home and didn't tell anyone about the incident, wishing it would just go away. Soon after, his Dad called my Dad, and then all hell broke loose. They wanted to talk with me and my father when they returned from the emergency room.

When they finally got back and we went over to their house, my friend's Dad was so angry with me that he wanted to do the punishing. He wanted to give me a hard spanking. My Mom and Dad were extremely upset over me taking my stabbing fantasy out on a neighbor boy. I felt terrible too, and knew I was going to be in big-time trouble with the county and my social worker. This act of violence pretty well cured me of my fascination with knives.

(Derek Clark)

Anger, Violence & Responsibility

Interview Between Shelly Bonnah & Derek Clark

January 30, 2012

Shelly: So you weren't violent in a way that you would describe like 'I see red...I'm out-of-control'. You chose violence?

Derek: Definitely. I trusted my power. I never zoned out. I did what I wanted to do. If I wanted to break a window or break something out of anger, that's exactly what I did. I made the choice. It was never like zoning out and then wake back up to reality and be like "what did I do?" If I got in a fight with somebody, I trusted that I could beat their ass. I believed in myself, whether it was bad or good. I made the choice that I wanted to make. I was big into independence and control. Looking back at all the fights I was in I can tell you that it was the younger Derek looking for a way to let out my pain. It was the only way that I knew that felt like I was making a statement that "I hate my life. I hate everyone and do not try to control me or push me around." I really needed some creative outlets to let out some steam and let me find a creative way to express my inner pain instead of taking it out on the world, foster parents, pastors, teachers etc.

Shelly: That makes sense to me. Do you know why?

Derek: Because acting out in rage is a choice and I made my choice.

Shelly: And because if you have the ability to choose to be violent, as I believe people do, you have the same ability to chose **not** to be. And that's exactly what you did a little later in life...?

Derek: Yes and there's a part of trust right there, right? Because you trust your choices. Even though I knew it was a bad choice and everyone had tried hard to tell me to control myself over the years, I still decided to make the choice that everyone didn't want me to make. It was a way for me to be in control of Derek and a way for me to do what I wanted to do and basically say 'screw you' to the adults. I definitely was a rebel. It was my way and I was not going to care what the adults thought because I didn't care about them. I felt as if everyone was trying to box me in so this was a way for me to blow the box up...with rage and poor choices and tell everyone to back the hell off me. Unfortunately with that kind of thinking, you do hurt many people who are cheering you on. I definitely self-sabotaged myself so many times just because I could—as a statement to others.

This is my spirit—a fighter! My foster parents will tell you that and they will also tell you that I came to their house not able to really feel physical pain. I could turn off that part of my brain and simply not "feel". I was very numb. I seriously was just an angry little boy with no hope, no love and feeling like no one cared.

Yes, I was the middle child. My mom had her "special" daughter. Having a daughter of my own, I know that little girls can be so different than little boys. My mom dropped out of school in the eighth grade and really didn't know much about dealing with simple or critical issues. She once said to me that she had this 'perfect little girl' and then here I came...a devil...just an angry spirit basically...a violent little spirit...came right out of the womb like that. That's why she believed I was a devil. It is obvious that I was so different from my sister...

Shelly: You had been surrounded by violence before you had even been born...

Derek: Yes, My mom told me that when she was 7 months pregnant with me, my dad came into the diner where she was waitressing and took her to the back in the kitchen and threw her down to the ground and continued to stomp, kick and hit her stomach. She believed he was trying to kill me right there...but you know...I Lived!

Shelly: You wouldn't have survived if you didn't come out a fighter...

Derek: Yes, what a crazy guy my dad was. Did you know that they found my dad when I was 6 years old? He was at Folsom State Prison for the criminally insane for a series of armed robberies from Arizona to California. The closest I have been to him is when I was looking at my county foster care files a few years ago and I noticed a page where he signed over his guardian/parental rights to the state. I felt a sense of acceptance that he did the right thing by never coming back for me. It was there in black and white, my dad giving up on me...but I am grateful for him not fighting it and doing the right thing. From what I've heard, my dad was crazy!

Shelly: So...If we look at the whole picture here...it really wouldn't have made any sense any other way had you not been born a warrior, you wouldn't have survived.

Derek: Yeah there is a good chance that I would have not survived, but I have met so many other youth in care that have gone through much worse than I did and yet may not have that fighting spirit but rather a spirit of sadness and depression. I am grateful for my fighting spirit...that dogged will within that kept me fighting and pushing forward; to never give up and to never take no for an answer and do it my way.... maybe not the smartest or easiest way, but I did it my way.

Shelly: And had you not actually been a pretty tough kid, it's hard to say what would have happened...but we're talking about a difference here between a 'warrior' and a 'perpetrator', someone who intentionally overpowers another person with the intention of harming them, like you're describing your dad.

Derek: Yes, I agree. I would have turned out so different and maybe done some really cowardly things like killing another person. It actually takes more courage to just walk away than to hurt another person or animal. I had a foster brother that would get mad at my foster parents, then go out on the farm, and hurt the animals. It was awful. I thought of him as a coward. Take responsibility for your life and own your life. Accept the consequences of your actions and change your life accordingly, instead of taking an animal's life out of anger or taking another person's life out of anger. Some people can't, or won't, control themselves. They are NOT fighters, they are cowards and it goes on from there to rape and molestation. I have heard so many stories on how these kids of this world have been abused in every crazy way possible by a parent, priest, uncle, grandpa, teacher, coach, neighbor, stepdad, etc. And those victims of abuse fight to take their life back and to try to heal so that their perpetrator does not control their mind and heart throughout their life.

I believe we are all born fighters, I mean we had to fight to come into this world through that little birth canal and then somewhere along the way, some lose their fight for life and end up fighting their way through foster care. I have personally lived it and have forgiven my own mother. She was about 70 years old when she finally was able to give me a meaningful apology. She used to say to me when I was always looking for a 'sorry' from her, "hey you turned out alright". What was that supposed to mean? Feel good, respected, valued, validated and acknowledged? Well guess what, it didn't. I needed the real deal, the word "Sorry".

Shelly: And…because of your heart, your personality, because of your spirit, and your self-control and your trust in yourself you were able to manage all of that well enough so that you chose to stop hurting people. You didn't go to jail…you had all this control to manage it so that you didn't do any life-altering harm to anybody including yourself. So that's a pretty amazing story, actually. These are the things that you have uniquely figured out in order to not only maintain power in your life, but dignity…

Derek: Yes. You know, looking at those psychological and speech and language reports, I am shocked on how quickly they packaged me and labeled me. I love that quote that says, "Once you label me, you negate me." We cannot just give in to the easy method of labeling, packaging and now try to send a person off. I am an individual, not just a number! Although I did have a lot of behavior problems, it came with the abuse, neglect and lack of value that was placed upon my little self at that time. What a lot to handle. Seriously, you want to know what got me through all this crap in my life? It was my personal belief that I was a super hero. Seriously! The incredible hulk or superman or the million-dollar man. I believed I had power and they called it 'withdrawn from reality' and 'erratic psychosis'. I felt I was powerful from the beginning, and I would inflict negative power because they were negative to me or abuse me. Whether it was behavior with feces and urine or hurting somebody, I've always had it. I've learned how to harness it and use it to my advantage. Some people don't learn that. I will get what I want in life. I've had the advantages of never being put on medication as a kid and never becoming controlled by drugs and alcohol. I need all of my senses—I would never give that away to drugs or alcohol. I can't control a lot of circumstances, I know that, but I can control my attitude and I can control the way I think.

An Assessment Lens
Instant Message

1. Drugs, sometimes major tranquilizers, act by numbing brain cells to surges of dopamine, a chemical that has been linked to euphoria and psychotic delusions. This approach masks the grief and trauma associated with family separations and other forms of adversity.

2. Resistance is any mental or behavioral act through which a person attempts to expose, withstand, repel, stop, prevent, abstain from, strive against, impede, refuse to comply with, or oppose any form of violence or oppression (including any type of disrespect), or the conditions that make such acts possible. This is healthy. Sometimes youth in care are resisting 'the system' itself.

3. Resistance that takes the form of violence is intentional and youth can, and should, be held fully responsible for their acts of violence. Formulating responses as resistance does not negate accountability in favor of compassionate understanding.

EXERCISE

Think back to a time in your life when you faced a specific situation of violence, adversity or oppression.

a) What was <u>going through your mind</u> to expose, withstand, repel, stop, prevent, abstain from, strive against, impede, or refuse to comply with what was happening to you?

b) What were you <u>doing</u> to expose, withstand, repel, stop, prevent, abstain from, strive against, impede, or refuse to comply with what was happening to you?

Resistance cannot be judged by its effectiveness in stopping abuse, violence, or situations of trauma. It is, however, ever-present and universal in the preservation of safety and dignity.

Chapter Six: Watch Your Language; Words that Kill the Spirit

When you're guarded, and your walls are up, you don't want to let your walls down because you've lived most of your life with them up. That's how I protect myself. That's how I've protected myself for a long time.

(Derek Clark)

[Derek] AS YOU can see from the reports, a lot of effort was put into describing my personality and mental capacity. One of the most disturbing words the doctor used was "retarded." Of any word used to describe me over the years, this is the one that I struggle with the most. This word, and others that are equally definitive, are extremely harmful to kids. What we think we can become, we usually become or what we hear you say, we have a greater chance of growing into. If a child is repeatedly minimized and labeled, we believe he or she will lose the will to try—the will to exceed what is expected of them. Yes, I had delayed development and yes, I had extreme emotional problems. As we have described throughout this book, there are understandable explanations for both my developmental delays and my emotional responses to the circumstances of my life in terms of both the trauma that I endured, and the social responses that I received. If, alternatively, labels are hastily assigned as an explanation to a child's development and behavioral responses, he or she is at great risk of growing into that label—becoming the disorder itself. This applies not only to children of all ages, but adults as well. We hear evidence of this throughout a variety of reports about children and youth, on referral forms and through the verbal exchanges between professionals.

Words have the power to make kids feel like lesser beings. Even when kids joke about being a "retard" or say "I am dumb," or, "I can't do that," it gradually instills that negativity in their minds; in fact it becomes 'truth' and identity forming. Their mental hard drive is being programmed, and these labels and words become difficult to erase. If we contribute to the assimilation of these limiting, destructive words, we contribute to children and youth believing their own messages.

I may never know how my foster parents were able to see me differently than the ways in which I was described, and in fact the ways in which I often behaved. The words from the reports that we are highlighting in this chapter ran through their hands, perhaps numerous times; and yet they held their belief in me as someone who would become great one day. I behaved disrespectfully, aggressively, and violently, and they responded with a swift and certain consequence followed with the words *"Derek, you are better than this"*. Beyond a shadow of a doubt, I knew that they meant it. I didn't always believe it myself, but I knew that they did. The descriptions that follow were completely unknown to me until I was about 12 or 13 years old and my foster parents were going out for the evening. I remember hearing them say to the babysitter "don't allow Derek to go into the filing cabinet inside the closet." Curiosity struck me, and I had to find a way to get the babysitter distracted. I successfully had her pre-occupied and I carefully opened the closet and started pulling out the drawers of the 4-foot filing cabinet. As I quickly looked at each file label, I found that there was a file on 'Derek Clark.' I pulled it out carefully and I saw a drawing that I had done in elementary school, report cards, and then a bunch of paperwork that I didn't have time to go through, but it looked very important. As I was going through the papers quickly, I saw highlighted in yellow "mentally retarded". I could not believe it. I double-checked the paper to make sure it had my name on it, and it did. I was in shock. I then continued to read the highlighted areas. I can't remember what else it said. I put everything back in the filing cabinet, closed the closet doors and held onto my secret for a while. I was shocked that I was labeled mentally retarded when I knew I was not. I did not discuss it with anyone. At that point, I had been finished with psychiatric counseling. I had been going to counseling twice a week for about 6 years and it was never brought up. I eventually had the courage to share it with my foster mom and dad they said..."oh Derek, we didn't believe those reports. We knew you were not retarded when we got you." My foster parents were both teachers and obviously very wise to not share with me the labels that the psychiatrist, neurologist and speech and language evaluator had placed up on me in the system. I am eternally grateful that they never gave in to the labels and instead they treated me like a kid who was grieving.

Here are the words that described me over a number of years, categorically rejected by my foster parents:

➢ *The minor's behavior has grown virtually unmanageable....*

➢ *The boy is hyperactive...*

➢ *When he becomes involved in an activity, which might endanger him or others around him, he will not respond to reasonable directions to stop this negative type of behavior...*

➢ *The minor must be physically restrained and he flies into rages and is completely unmanageable...*

> *The minor has been observed to pound his head on the floor...*

> *The mother is fearful of hitting the child and injuring him...*

> *The minor must be supervised closely at all times...*

> *Derek is hyperactive and emotionally disturbed...*

> *Derek is unable to get along with anyone for any period of time...*

> *While the boy is not overtly psychotic, there is indication of this potential...*

> *The child laughs inappropriately and shows much anxiety...*

> *He is very suspicious of people and holds back as if fearful of making a mistake...*

> *The boy acts out against anyone around him...*

> *Derek talks frequently about guns, knives and hurting others...*

> *School placement should be carefully selected... this may be available through an educationally handicapped program.*

> *The Doctor feels there is mild retardation.*

As an adult it is painful to read the ways in which I was described as a young person who was in pain, abandoned, and excruciatingly frightened. It is also true that I became frightening for a period of time. Although that cannot be overlooked, minimized or excused, it also cannot become defining. I was always more than that. I made a conscious choice to not let these labels and opinions from others define me. The behaviors were my story that I didn't know how to tell, and my parents understood their job was about connection versus correction. Are we really connected to that child/youth? Have we collectively made a complete contribution to that child who is in the system as a result of the actions or circumstances of others? Have we spent the time to really get to know him or her in a way that gains insight into the private logic that drives their behavior? They don't do what they do for no reason, even if those reasons don't reveal themselves as logical or effective in the eyes of adults who have different lived experiences.

Medication

Interview Between Shelly Bonnah & Derek Clark

December 23, 2011

Shelly: What is your history with medication, considering the behavioral challenges that you presented as a young person?

Derek: It was recommended, but my foster parents wouldn't put me on any kind of drugs. Instead, they decided that they would work through the challenges with me by controlling my environment. I wasn't allowed soda, video games, fast food, sugar cereal, and I only got an hour of TV a week. They worked with me on my creative outlets, like music, sports, Scouts, 4H and church. They also worked on my character traits: integrity, responsibility, and hard work. They felt it was a better fit to work on my issues in a more natural way than with medication. Even now, I barely take Tylenol. At the age of 13 years old, I had a joint in my mouth, and something told me that if I smoked this, I was going to end up like my mom and dad. I took it out of my mouth and never had a problem with drugs or alcohol. I just don't like the idea of my brain being controlled by a substance.

It is interesting to know what these youth are feeling, thinking and believing underneath what they present to the world. I was recently speaking at a state foster youth conference. I spoke for about an hour and then I invited them to share their struggles with the audience. It was amazing to see the courage that they summoned to come up to the microphone and allow themselves to be witnessed by others. I made notes of the top 3 themes that emerged from their stories:

Number 1: "Why won't anyone listen to me? This is my life. No one will listen to me."

Number 2: "Why do I have to take medication? Why don't I have a choice?"

Number 3: "Why doesn't anyone ask me if I want to move, or where I want to go?"

These are compelling questions, and as the adults in the lives of children and youth in care, are we pausing long enough to reflect upon the answers?

[Shelly] Our attention to language in our work with children and youth is equivalent to the importance of how we consider power, oppression and safety. Our language will convey how we ethically and philosophically position ourselves, particularly when faced with situations of systemic oppression or violence. Dr. Vikki Reynolds (2010) has closely examined that which holds us together as professionals in the sustainability of community work. She has created a list of questions that invite the ongoing examination of our ethics, and we would like to close this chapter with an invitation to consider these questions as they pertain to our work with children and youth in the foster care system:

- ➤ How can we do justice working with people who struggle in the margins of our communities?
- ➤ How can we act in solidarity to keep the spirit of justice alive in our collective work and in our lives?
- ➤ How can we be connected with this aliveness?
- ➤ How can we hold on to our collective integrity and dignity?
- ➤ What ways can we find to sustain ourselves as community workers?
- ➤ How might work that develops richer understandings of social justice, and follows from commitments to social justice, be more sustaining than work that does not?
- ➤ How can we change the unjust structures that oppress people?
- ➤ What could just practice look like in a society which is more just to some than to others?

(Reynolds, 2010, p. 19)

Watch Your Language; Words that Kill the Spirit
Instant Message

1. If labels are hastily assigned as an explanation to a child's development and behavioral responses, he or she is at great risk of growing into that label—becoming the disorder itself.

2. The behaviors are a story that children and youth may not be able to tell any other way, and foster caregivers can understand their job is to focus on connection verses correction.

3. [Derek Clark] The words from the reports that we are highlighting in this chapter ran through their hands, perhaps numerous times; and yet they held their belief in me as someone who would become great one day. I behaved disrespectfully, aggressively, and violently, and they responded with a swift and certain consequence followed with the words *"Derek, you are better than this"*.

4. The 3 themes presented by youth in care at a Derek Clark conference:

Number 1: "Why won't anyone listen to me? This is my life. No one will listen to me".

Number 2: "Why do I have to take medication? Why don't I have a choice?"

Number 3: "Why doesn't anyone ask me if I want to move, or where I want to go?"

EXERCISE

Pause for a moment to consider the most recent interaction that you had with a child or youth in care. What do you recall about what happened? Now consider how much of your attention he or she had (60%, 75%, 90%?). Is there anything from that interaction that you want to revisit?

Chapter Seven: Mad & Sad; Grief
Understood as behavior disorders

I am a fighter by nature and early on showed signs of stubbornness in doing what I wanted and refusing to acknowledge another's opinion of me. This tendency has carried on throughout my life. I do everything "Derek's way." I felt like the world was against me and that nobody liked me. I felt like I was totally backed into a corner, and the only way for me to let others know I was a real kid was to come out swinging.

(Derek Clark)

[Shelly] EVERY CHILD living under government care has a story of loss. An inherent reality of being in care creates a severed, ruptured, or disrupted connection to their families of origin. For those who have experienced multiple foster home placements, multiple stories of loss and/or trauma exist. An alternative view to 'youth mental illness' is describing the defiance and oppositional behavior of kids in care as 'intelligence gathering'. This is a process where they use what is most readily available to them—their behavior—to test, push, trick and challenge the unfamiliar people and environments that have entered their lives. Youth learn to accurately assess their environment while responding to the numerous threats they perceive around them.

Distractibility may be exposed as grief; this can look strikingly similar to ADHD or ADD and is frequently treated with stimulant medication.

Derek: As a kid, I never went the path of depression. I was mainly the class clown and then could switch in an instant to the guy out of control, and then the fighter. I would not take anything from anyone, never. If somebody came at me with what I thought was disrespect or telling me what to do, adult or youth, I would take the challenge on and explode on them verbally or physically. I also a very hyperactive little boy, very fidgety, with severe anxiety and very suspicious of others. I would act out to try to shock them and throw them off on purpose. I would even try to shock the therapists by my reactions just to throw them off their game. To me, it was an even bigger game…

Shelly: Throughout your time growing up, were you 'out' about being a foster kid or was that hidden?

Derek: I kept that pretty much hidden. No one really knew. I never started off a conversation like "hey, I am a foster kid was thrown away and now I have a foster home because I was a reject." I felt a lot of shame about it. It definitely was not a conversation starter. I was my little secret and if you knew, you probably found out through my foster parents, foster brother or foster sister. I never liked talking about it. I probably covered it up with the violence and being a clown. Even into early adulthood I wouldn't openly admit that I was ever a foster kid.

Aggression may be exposed as fear; fear disguised as aggression can be difficult to recognize. These kids are often terrified.

Shelly: What about fear?

Derek: My foster parents will tell you I never had fear. I had the mental capability to block out fear. I was able to compartmentalize, file it way in my head and move on. It was nothing I ever felt. And so it's gone into my adulthood with no fear of taking action...no fear of jumping off the ledge of life's creative world and going after my dreams. I look at the world through creative eyes and know that I have the power to accomplish anything I put my heart, mind and soul to. Anxiety? Yes. But fear? No problem there.

I think that it is normal to have this kind of fear though... one thing I'm fearful of is something happening to my kids or me dying too early and not being around for my kids.

I have had nightmares that will try to plant seeds of fear within me. The nightmares were a reality though and then had to relive them when I went to sleep.

...As a kid, I did have a strong fear of the dark because of the images I had in my head...like when stepdad would hold my head in the toilet. As a kid, I was so scared of him...and then when I met him when I was 30 years old. Here I was 6 foot 5 inches and he was probably 5 feet 8 inches tall and weak looking. He wasn't a nightmare anymore.

...But typically...NO FEAR...

> **Humor may be exposed as a way of keeping people at bay;** commonly known as a class-clown, but serving a very specific purpose of distraction.

Shelly: You've mentioned being the class clown. What is the history of you using humor to get through situations in your life?

Derek: Yes, honestly, I would be a class clown! I would try to shock people from teachers, to pastors to my parent's friends to classes. I was all about getting attention. My foster parents will tell you "Derek would always try to shock people...just to get a reaction, by doing things out of the ordinary". It's probably my personality. That might be some of my blurts... those psychological evaluations said that "Derek blurts out stuff uncontrollably" (laughter)...so it's followed me into my adulthood.

Shelly: So that's one way of understanding it: "blurting things out uncontrollably". Another way of understanding it is learning at an early age how to distract people and how to get attention in exactly the way you wanted it in that moment...

Numbness as a way of moderating pain; this is not the same as dissociative disorder.

Derek: I was shutting down. That's how I do it. I was shutting down and I have the ability to just shut you out. I have an incredible ability to compartmentalize things in my brain like that.

Shelly: And you would be a master at it...you've developed this ability over the years to control what you are willing to feel, how much you will tolerate feeling it, and when...

Derek: Exactly.

Trusting would not be prudent where survival is at stake; this is not the same as an attachment disorder.

Shelly: How did you protect yourself emotionally in relationships as a kid?

Derek: Us foster kids always have an emotional back up plan because we don't know when we're going to get dropped or dumped or whatever. I always kept up a façade, a mask you know. Don't let anyone really know who you are.

Shelly: Ya...and yet the irony is that you're yearning for someone to know you for who you really are.

Derek: Yes. And I did try. But it was so difficult to be vulnerable enough to have a healthy relationship. It never really lasted. I pretty much sabotaged my own relationships.

High concentration on surroundings leaves minimal concentration available for school; this does not reflect on academic ability, but may speak to academic *availability.*

Shelly: What was it like for you to sit in a classroom throughout elementary school? High school?

Derek: I hated it and was bored constantly. I wanted to socialize with others.

Shelly: What did you find yourself doing if you were for some reason unable to socialize? Is that when you would do some work, or would you find something else to do?

Derek: It was hard for me to be quiet, so I would blurt out inappropriate comments to get some attention. I loved the attention. Unfortunately I got the wrong kind of attention and I was always in trouble.

Managing a complex environment makes honest relationships virtually impossible; this does not mean kids are 'liars'; they need help to manage the complexity of their lives.

Shelly: So you had all of these pieces of your life—nobody knew you were a foster child because you kept that pretty guarded, then you had all these appointments for various things, like social workers, psychiatrists, that nobody knew about—and you kept these things secret. And then you've got friendships that you maintained while keeping all these parts of your life secret. That strikes me as a lot to handle for a 10 year old kid.

Derek: Yes, I believe that it was my ability to not take life seriously. Everything is a joke and I will cause pain upon the world when I don't feel like joking around. I was a hot and cold kind of kid. I didn't have a depression issue where I was sad in a corner—I was more of a fighter trying to make my presence known. I didn't like people messing with me or questioning me.

Shelly: So if anyone questions you, or challenges you or teases you about the warts on your hands, about the fighting… about where you were…about your intelligence…about any of those things—you'd start swinging…the warrior came out to protect…

Derek: Most definitely!

A drop of longing says as much about the human spirit as a grand gesture of love or defiance.

(Allan Wade)

[Shelly] While youth are responding to fractured connections with their family, they are also being assessed, advised and responded to based on their 'behavior'. A Response-Based approach strives for the discovery of how youth experience, respond to and resist all of the circumstances in their lives. Most importantly, professionals can hold an assumption of youth mental wellness and health.

When the acts of resistance are recognized as defiance, such punitive measures as "refusing privileges, removing bedding and other things from their rooms...using chemical restraints...become accepted 'interventions' with youth in care (Lambe, National Youth In Care Network, 2006).

The primary relevance to youth is to be fully taken into account, deeply listened to and viewed as vigilantly committed to protecting their wellness, integrity and dignity. Increasingly, research has demonstrated the correlation between trauma and symptoms of behavioral and/or attachment disorders in children (Perry, 2006). The similarities between possible responses to traumatic experiences and some of the symptoms of Reactive Attachment Disorder, ADHD, and Major Depressive Disorder are demonstrated in the following charts:

Childhood Responses to Traumatic Experiences	DSM-IV Diagnosis Reactive Attachment Disorder
Daydreaming	Responds with frozen watchfulness
Numbness	Social relatedness is markedly disturbed
Distractibility	Ambivalent responses
'Head in the clouds'	Resistance to comforting
Inability to connect with others	Inability to form appropriate attachments

Childhood Responses to Traumatic Experiences	DSM-IV Diagnosis ADHD
Fidgeting	Squirms in Seat
Compulsive Talking	Talks Excessively
Darting eyes	Trouble Engaging
Anxiety	Appears 'driven'
Agitation	Trouble awaiting turn
Distractibility	Easily distracted
Out-of-Seat Behavior	Inappropriately leaves seat
Looking for a Fight	Interrupts

Childhood Responses to Traumatic Experience	DSM-IV Dagnosis Major Depressive Disorder
Feelings of helplessness	Feeling hopelessness, helpless, or worthless
Lack of initiative or motivation	Activity is sped up or slowed down
Listlessness	Tiredness or loss of energy
Failure to complete work	Impaired work function
Difficulty transitioning to new tasks	Trouble thinking or concentrating
Flat affect	Depressed mood
Sense of lifelessness	Repeated thoughts of suicide

The term 'trauma' is used to "refer to an emotional wound caused by a frightening and painful experience" (Webb, 2006). Clinical attention has primarily focused on the source *of* trauma, symptoms *of* trauma and treatment *to* trauma. A Response-Based approach is focused upon understanding first how individuals respond to, and intuitively resist traumatic experiences. These are experiences that assault a person's dignity, safety, and security. Secondly, what is the nature of social responses received by that individual following the traumatic experience—how did the people around him or her respond? In considering children and youth in foster care, how did they move between their biological home and a foster home? If they disclosed abuse, how were they responded to and what happened immediately following a disclosure? Who believes them and who doubts them? What is the response from their social worker, their parents, their foster parents, their friends, their school, and their neighbors? What were the risks involved with disclosure—the losses?

Ultimately, what determines how children survive trauma, physically, emotionally, or psychologically, is whether the people around them—particularly the adults they should be able to trust and rely upon—stand by them with love, support and encouragement. Fire can warm or consume, water can quench or drown, wind can caress or cut. And so it is with human relationships: we can both create and destroy, nurture and terrorize, traumatize and heal each other (Perry & Szalzvitz, 2006, p. 5).

Leading researcher on social responses, Sarah Ullman (2007), is demonstrating that the nature of positive or negative responses received by victims has a stronger correlation with recovery than the source of trauma itself.

Positive reactions of emotional support, tangible aid, and information support are helpful to survivors whether they come from formal or informal support providers. In contrast, negative reactions of blame, disbelief, and control are harmful from either source and may silence survivors and thwart help-seeking. Support sources must attempt to minimize their negative responses to victims and maximize positive responses to aid survivors' recovery (Ullman, 2007, p. 82)

The entry of a young person into care may be a result of a traumatic experience, and may in itself be a traumatic experience.

Regardless, by its very nature there is a disrupted connection from their family, neighborhood, school, and all that is familiar. There will very likely be an experience of grief. The following story provides an example of a positive social response to a traumatic experience.

I still remember the day as if it was yesterday; I was attending respite for the weekend. I had been bounced from home to home, half starved, ignored and neglected, unwanted and treated like a stray dog that you just 'tolerate', but never hit. Not til that warm summer day did I experience physical violence. I don't remember what we fought about, but I still remember the sound of the hard slap and me running out the screen door of the trailer in shock. I quickly ran several blocks away and sat on the large concrete plant holder at the local gas station. I probably sat there for at least an hour till a car pulled up beside me. It was my social worker who 'happened to be driving by' at the time. He got out slowly, came and sat down beside me, and looked up towards the mountains, saying nothing at first. He then tilted his head down, and while fidgeting with his hands asked me what I was doing out here. I turned my head to look at him; the tears I shed were mostly dry by now. I told him "she hit me". He said nothing as the statement sunk in. We sat quietly for a minute until he said "let's get you out of here".

Shane Dobratz (28), Former Youth in Care

The loss associated with moving from a family of origin to a foster family is defined as circumstantial loss (Lendrum & Syme, 2002, p. 73). Unlike the tasks described within the mourning process (Worden, 2002, p. 27) in the event of death, circumstantial loss is far less recognized and is "simply disregarded by adults through encouraging the children to think only of the gain" (Lendrum & Syme, 2002, p. 74). Further to this, children do not have the resources or experience to integrate loss into their world (Kubler-Ross & Kessler, 2005). In their minds they often fill in gaps with thoughts like "It must somehow be *my* fault...they are the forgotten grievers" (p.160). The emphasis that we place on experiences of loss is not intended to minimize other significant experiences of adversity that children and youth are faced with. Rather, we suggest that the range of adverse events experienced by kids in care concurrently contain strong elements of loss. For example, violence introduces a loss of safety; neglect inherently creates a loss of nurturing, and abuse sets up a loss of trust. These losses, similar to physical separation, create particular and specific responses from children that will not be revealed through a lens of the 'effects' of violence, neglect and abuse.

Dr. Francine Cournos, a psychiatrist, describes her personal experience of profound grief and loss while growing up within the foster care system. She recognizes that "traumatized children are also bereaved. They need to grieve their losses, even if what is lost was insufficient, such as in situations of danger, abuse, or neglect, before meaningful new attachments are possible" (2002, p. 140). Corresponding to this are the views of Anderson and Seita (2006), who note, "In the child welfare system, by definition, the initial source of a child's trauma is a parent". Grief, loss and trauma are not interchangeable terms; Cournos explains that the factors making childhood loss traumatic is the feeling of having been betrayed by trusted adults (2002). Cournos describes her own experience as one of powerlessness, and the only power she had left was the power to say "NO" (2007, personal communication).

Bonding ruptures create specific responses from children in their attempts to regain predictability, which are well documented in research conducted around childhood attachment (Bowlby, 1969/1989). When a child's need for safety, either emotional or physical, is such that a system of professional caregivers is introduced into their lives, grief processes can become complicated with the overlay of further traumatic experiences. This makes it increasingly important to appreciate the complexity and depth of children's ties to their caregivers (Jones & Kruk, 2005).

> Trauma occurs when a serious threat presents itself, but action is of no avail—neither resistance nor escape is possible. The ordinary ways of coping become overwhelmed, disorganized, and fragmented. Systems of attachment and meaning are disrupted. Faith in life's order and continuity is lost and the world becomes unsafe (Cournos, 2006, p. 107).

The benefits associated with deepening our understanding of the role played by social responses could unilaterally shape the positive interactions between professionals and children in care.

Social Responses

Interview Between Shelly Bonnah & Derek Clark

February 15, 2012

Shelly: You mentioned respite? How did you experience living with one family, and going to stay with another family some of the time? How was it explained to you?

Derek: I went to people who were part of my foster parents' inner circle, from church, so I didn't have a problem with it. I considered them my aunt and uncle.

There would be times when I would stay with my aunt and uncle because my foster family would go to my grandma's house. They wouldn't take me because my foster grandma wouldn't accept that I was their "real" kid so she didn't acknowledge me.

Shelly: Can you say more about that?

Derek: My foster mom talked to me about it and made me feel better. She said that her parents were losing out. So basically when they went to visit the grandparents, I would stay at my parents good friends who we considered them aunt and uncle.

I remember this one Christmas where my foster mom's parents bought presents for everyone else but me because I was not their "real" grandchild. It is kind of crazy when you think about it. I would never do that. As an adult, I would think you would have compassion and empathy for that little kid. Finally my foster mom did say to her mom and dad that they had to buy family gifts instead of individual because it's not fair to Derek.

Shelly: How did you know all of that was going on?

Derek: Cause I remember not getting a gift from "*grandma*" like everyone else.

Shelly: What did you think about it at the time? What was going through your mind?

Derek: I thought it was mean. I knew that grandma just didn't like me. I never had a relationship with her ever...ever.

But my mom finally put her foot down and said, "that's not fair to Derek".

Shelly: And your mom told you that she said that?

Derek: Yes, because we had a talk about it. How her mom was mean.

Shelly: And she agreed with you, about how her mom was mean?

Derek: Yes, she thought it was very unfair. Because I wasn't their real kid. But…um…I didn't care about them anyways…

Shelly: Well…sounds like you didn't know them and they didn't know you. But it sends a message, right? It's not the people that would matter so much, but the message matters a great deal, don't you think?

Derek: Yes, another person who rejected me. Kinda like a sense of abandonment, almost, even though they didn't matter to me.

Shelly: That message can get inside you, if you're not paying attention…

Derek: Yes…how awful to not get a gift when everyone else gets a gift. It tells you you're not as good as them and that you are a nothing to them.

No Self-worth
No Self-value
No Self-esteem
I'm not good enough
I'm not a real kid

Mad & Sad; Grief Understood as behavior disorders
Instant Message

1. **Distractibility may be exposed as grief;** this can look strikingly similar to ADHD or ADD and is frequently treated with stimulant medication.

2. **Aggression may be exposed as fear;** fear disguised as aggression can be difficult to recognize. These kids are often terrified.

3. **Trusting would not be prudent where survival is at stake;** this is not the same as an attachment disorder.

4. **High concentration on surroundings leaves minimal concentration available for school;** this does not reflect on academic ability, but may speak to academic *availability.*

5. **Managing a complex environment makes honest relationships virtually impossible;** this does not mean kids are 'liars'; they need help to manage the complexity of their lives.

Chapter Eight: Finding the Leader Within

Written for Youth

> One of the most important lessons I have learned in life is not to let my past infect my future.
>
> **(Derek Clark)**

[Derek] THIS CHAPTER is about choice. One of the most important lessons I have learned in life is not to let my past infect my future. Think about some time in your life, a time that has been really tough to overcome. Or think about some troubling event you keep dwelling on. What happens while you're dwelling on the past is that you become so obsessively fixated on a particular incident that it hinders you from moving forward with your life. Having the ability to learn from the past, and let things go, is what it takes to develop into a leader. This isn't always easy, I understand. I have let the pain of my past infect my future at times, and it has certainly held me back. I've been lost, not knowing what direction to take in my life. There have been times when all I could think was, "Why me?" But you must understand that this way of thinking, this fixation on the negative, will almost certainly ensure that your future will be filled with more of the same.

Your parent's mistakes, or your own mistakes for that matter, don't have to define the person you are. Don't let your mistakes or your parent's mistakes define you or confine you, but rather, let them refine you. I realized as a young man that I didn't have to feel guilty and blame myself any longer for the pain my mother, father, and other people caused me. I had to take responsibility for my own life and not let any other person control my heart and mind. It was time for me to take leadership over my own life. I needed to unload this twenty-thousand-pound backpack of emotional distress, anger, rage, and sense of being valueless. No longer was I going to suffer at the hands of others' past mistakes, or even my own. I realized that I wanted to be a victor in life and no longer a victim. I wanted to ROCK!

There is a simple formula that I have used to bring more meaning into my life. It is a program I teach when I do seminars. It is called I-R.O.C.K. It is an acronym for how I live my life, as well as how I inspire others to live theirs:

I = Integrity

R = Responsibility

O = Opportunity

C = Choice

K = Knowledge

Integrity

INTEGRITY CAN be measured by how well you live up to your own principles and values. Often we fail to meet our own standards and expectations, but if we give it our best shot, our integrity remains intact. That part of yourself, this person who holds you accountable to a higher standard, is the person who assesses your integrity. This is who you are when the lights go out and you are alone with your own conscience. You cannot hide from yourself. Integrity is about being honest in your dealings with both others and yourself. Integrity concerns what people think about you when you are not around – your reputation. It's about how people perceive you, and what message you are sending to others about your character. This is also how you perceive yourself. Do you hold yourself up with dignity? Do you have respect for yourself and others? Having integrity is about sending a message to your family, friends and coworkers – now and in the future - -that you are truthful and reliable. What you expect from others you should also expect from yourself.

> *"The ideas that have lighted my way have been kindness, beauty and truth."- Albert Einstein*

Responsibility

RESPONSIBILITY IS what determines whether your life is more about being a victim or more about being a victor. Developing the ability to take responsibility for your words, thoughts, actions and emotions will change the quality of your life. This is your life, and you have to take responsibility for it. This means being accountable for your actions and words. I believe a big part of taking responsibility is releasing the poison in your heart. The only way to do that is to forgive. Forgiving others who have done you wrong, and forgiving yourself are both crucial to achieving a happy life. I know from experience. I was poisoning my life by not letting go of earlier pain. If you need assistance from others to do this effectively—get it. The help is available to you if you are willing to accept it.

As a teenager, I used to walk through life with a giant chip on my shoulder. I was mad at everyone who I felt was against me. And if you weren't for me, you were against me, in my mind. I was disrespectful to other people and to anybody who was an authority. Part of my problem was that I was not taking complete responsibility for the direction of my life. I was used to blaming others for my situation and the way I was. I blamed my Mom for giving me up and keeping my brother and sister. I blamed my Dad for not caring about his own son. I blamed my foster parents because at times I felt like they prohibited me from going home to my biological mother, even though that wasn't a rational or logical thought.

I have had to learn and relearn that you can't believe everything you think. Every thought that comes into your mind must be filtered. You have to ask yourself whether a thought contributes positively or negatively to your life. Is it a negative, toxic voice that wants to attach itself to your brain, and eventually take over your heart and soul? I often believed that everyone was out to hurt me, and it was this thought that made me the way I was. Blaming others will only stop you from really enjoying life. You start to think that everyone is out to get you in some way, when in reality all that is hurting you is your own attitude. Make a commitment right now. Tell yourself that you are going to take responsibility for your life. You are going to get back up, dust yourself off, and be stronger and wiser. This is your life! If you don't take responsibility for it, who will? Start today, so you don't have any regrets for wasted yesterdays.

"You cannot escape the responsibility of tomorrow by evading it today." - Abraham Lincoln

Opportunity

OPPORTUNITY IS your chance to have exactly what you want in life. Opportunity may seem like a hidden thing, or something vague. But the good thing about opportunity is that it's always right there in front of you, ready for you to reach out and grab it! And once you get a hold if it, it will change your life. Many people take full advantage of this fact - the nearness of opportunity. They wait for the opportunities to come to them. In reality, 99% of the time you have to go out and look for it. Once you find it, don't be afraid to go for it! I believe the reason people don't look for opportunities that could make their life better is fear. Fear of the unknown, fear of failure, the fear of what people will think of them. This is your life and you had better make the most of it.

This is the true meaning of my sayings, Never Give Up and Never Limit Your Life. You have to trust yourself! You must know and believe that you have to explore every opportunity that may contribute to the fulfillment of your dreams, to your job, to your schooling, and everything else in life. There have been many, many people who did something great with their life simply because they had the courage to take a chance, a risk. By risking much, we are often led to opportunities we may never have imagined, or even dreamed of, had we been more timid. I believe success comes when you try to go for as many opportunities as you can. Do this, and you continually push yourself forward in life. There is nothing wrong with failure. Every person who has done something great has met with failure. If you don't try, you will eventually collect so many regrets over wasted yesterdays that you won't have the happy and fulfilling life you might have had – the life that you deserve! So go for it, take a chance…

> *"Chance never helps those who do not help themselves." – Sophocles*

Choice

CHOICE IS probably the biggest factor in whether you are going to live a happy and fulfilling life. Everything in life revolves around a choice. It doesn't matter who you are; you could be the wealthiest or the poorest person on Earth. It doesn't matter where you live; you could live in Lithuania or Tasmania or Kentucky. Your age doesn't matter; you can be young or old. Who we are as individuals is just the sum of the choices we've made. Our first and most important choice concerns our attitude toward life - how do we respond to the world at large? Be grateful for this time we've been given on Earth, and everything else will fall into place. Even the challenges can bring great happiness, if we respond positively to life. Problems can be temporary if we don't attach ourselves to them and make them part of our identity.

Everything in your life is a choice. Even when you don't make a choice, you are really choosing to not choose! This may seem silly, but it is actually a very important idea. If we are always making a choice, even when choosing not to choose, why not instead become an active chooser? Your choices determine your character – wouldn't you prefer to be self-determined?

Making the right choice is a courageous act, but we often make the wrong ones. But thankfully, with every choice we make in life, whether good or bad, there is something to learn. Certain choices bring punishments, while others bring happiness and peace. I have made choices that have affected other people's happiness. I often chose to be disrespectful, hurt people's feelings, and hurt myself. But instead of choosing to dwell on my past mistakes and be destroyed by guilt, I chose to stop going down the self-destructive path I was on. I also made the choice to rid myself of all my negative feelings, and to look at life from a different perspective. Making the right choice over the wrong has immediate rewards, and you will notice them.

I also chose to learn from my poor choices. For so long, I was making one poor choice after another, until I realized I was miserable and wanted a happier life. More importantly, it dawned on me that it was all my choice. I had the power to change direction. As soon as I figured out that little secret, my ability to make wiser choices became more conscious and self-directed. I grew wiser, and began to really contemplate my actions and reasons for them. I realized that up to then I'd made decisions based on a reactionary relationship to life. Life would come at me, and I would react. How much better to push back on the world than have it pushing against you! Once decisions become a matter of conscious choice, and not a matter of simply reacting to outside forces, it totally opens up the field of options. You realize that you have tons of choices that will help you better your life. You may have felt trapped because the world was pressing in on you – but there are endless opportunities once you realize you are free to direct your own will.

Now I desire to make more wise and thoughtful moves. To make the choices that will better my life, instead of help destroy it. As a teenager, you are in a very difficult position. Every day you are faced with many choices to make, and they come at you from all sides. There are people pushing drugs your way, cigarettes, alcohol, gangs and sex. There are people pushing you to do what it takes to try to be popular, or to have certain attitudes that they think are cool. You have pressure to get good grades from one quarter, and bad grades from another. You may have a boyfriend or girlfriend and parents aren't going to approve of them. People may think you spend too much time on the phone, the internet, and texting. You may have pressure to respect or disrespect your parents, tell the truth or tell lies.

All these things add up to an immense amount of pressure, and sometimes your life literally hangs in the balance.

Making a poor choice could result in major consequences, punishment, or death. So be wise when making your choices. Adolescence is the practice ground for decision-making. It's there so that when you become an adult, living on your own, you will have gotten a lot of learning out of the way and will know how to spot the difference between a wise choice and a poor one. You can focus on choices that are going to improve your life financially, socially, spiritually, and physically.

> *"You must give up the way it is... to have it the way you want it, it's a choice."* -Unknown

Knowledge

KNOWLEDGE IS essential at every stage of life. Knowledge will always give you more options. The more you learn, the more you will grow. If I could push you in any direction, I would say: *GO TO COLLEGE!* Looking back, I wish I had gone to college - but I took a different road. If I had gone to college, I know that I would have been smarter in business, which has been a big part of my life. I had to learn some hard lessons.

Always seek advice when you make big decisions from people who have knowledge that you trust. One of my friends passed on some great advice to me: "Derek, when you want make a big decision, check with three of your smartest friends." Always make sure you have friends who are smarter than you. These are the people who will help you rise to their level. In high school I didn't hang out with the academic scholars; I mainly hung out with the academically challenged! Now I try to have friends who are smarter than me in areas where I am lacking knowledge. And in the spirit of generosity, I hope that I am a useful friend to others in areas where I have gained knowledge that they need. Friendships should be a healthy balance.

Knowledge is so important to helping catapult dreams into reality. But I also believe that knowledge should go hand-in-hand with imagination. Knowledge can have limits, whereas imagination is completely unlimited. But knowledge will help guide your imagination; controlling and containing it in such a way that it leads to something tangible you can give the world.

Imagine if I became what I've always dreamed about - let's say, for example, I was a professional songwriter. Well, I wouldn't be a very good songwriter if I didn't learn about different types of music, notes, syncopation, tone, melody, timing, rests, and other aspects of music theory. If I didn't know any of that, I would probably end up writing songs that no one would want to hear. Suppose you wanted to be a doctor. You would have to go to school for many years, and then do your residency – basically, learning on the job and applying what you were taught in school. The more you exercise your intelligence and expand your knowledge, the more information you have to make the educated decisions that will impact your life.

Do not be afraid to ask questions! How else are you going to learn and process what you need to know? Ask and be curious. In life, everything you do or don't do is processed in your brain. Your brain labels and stores it. Make sure you are taking in as much information as you can about different cultures, art, music, travel, education, religions, political views, foods, etc.… The more information you have, the greater your understanding will be. If we had more people interested in gathering good information, we would have a lot less ignorance about each other and our differences. We can learn from others all about the different ways of approaching the world. Then, we can choose which bits we want to apply in our own life. Knowledge is power - now go get some!

Let me end on this note. You have all that it takes to claim victory in your life. You have the looks, the talent, the attitude, the desire and the power to create the life you have always imagined. If you haven't imagined what kind of life you want as an adult, you had better start thinking about it. It is better to be prepared than to be scared. Life is about learning and growing every day. Follow your dreams and follow your heart, because your life is going to follow after your thoughts. Today is the day you decide that U ROCK!

"He who asks a question is a fool for a minute; he who does not remains a fool forever." — *Chinese Proverb*

I want to point out some things I have learned from learning about leadership. I have learned that there are two different kinds of leaders. One who leads for the good, and one who leads for the bad. The worst kind of leaders this world has seen have been those who lead through anger and intimidation. In order for you to be an effective leader, you must first lead yourself. You have to first be a worthy example, so that others will want to follow you. You have to show that you have the skills to lead yourself before you can lead others.

Now here are the qualities of a great leader!

L - Learns how to turn their weaknesses into their strengths

E - Ethical - Encourages others to succeed - Enthusiastic

A - Appreciates others - Action-Taker - great Attitude - Acknowledges others

D - Determined - never gives up without a fight

E - Example to follow- Empathetic, understands others

R - Responsible - Reliable - Ready to act with strength and courage

These are great traits to take on and develop. Remember, leadership begins with leadership over you. Act towards yourself the way you would towards the people you might lead. I know that if you take on these traits, your life will be happier, and people will want to be around you. People naturally gravitate towards great leaders. You'll radiate an exciting energy, and you'll train yourself to exhibit the self-discipline and control necessary to march bravely through the rough patches in life. A great leader also remains calm in times of adversity.

You have within you so much potential! Every one of us has the potential to become a great leader. It is your choice. If you follow the I-R.O.C.K. principals, you will find it much easier to conduct your life in a productive and influential way. A great leader can turn hopelessness into the power of hope by encouraging others. Once you help others find hope, they will in turn share it with others. It becomes a ripple effect, continually moving forward, until many people feel the positive vibe. I have had the great opportunity to lead others to success. As a leader, I have been tested by life's many hardships. These trials and hard times allowed me opportunities to shine, thrive, and become a stronger person. I chose to learn from the hard times. You too have the ability to be a courageous, strong, successful, and great leader! You can achieve your wildest dreams. Believe me, you have what it takes!

Recommendations & Parting Words

> Every one of you has greatness. You were born with it.
>
> (Derek Clark)

[Shelly] The decision to have a child or youth leave a foster home cannot be minimized as one that is flippantly made by caregivers or made based on minor issues. What is missing from the one-dimensional statistics of youth in care moving from home to home is the arduous decision-making process that is seldom made in isolation. These decisions are generally based on the belief that either the home is not adequately equipped for the child, the child is unhappy in the home, or some combination of both. In the most treacherous circumstances, a foster home is deemed unsafe for children. The fact remains, regardless of the pain involved for both youth and caregivers in the process of letting kids go, foster kids are moving from home to home within the system of government care at an alarming rate. These statistics vary between Canada and the United States, however, what is consistent is that it is rare for a child to remain in one home as Derek Clark did. What has also become commonly known, and increasingly so, is that moving from home to home hurts kids, regardless of the circumstances or justifications. With every move there is loss, and with loss there is grief.

The Response-Based approach is introduced to provide a framework that will guide professionals through respectful and dignity-preserving dialogue and social responses with children and youth. Most importantly, it will promote professional attitudes of hope, equality, acceptance and compassion. The Model for Sustainable Wellness includes understanding the context of events through asking direct questions to elicit an individual's unique experience, the meaning that they attribute to that experience, how they respond to, and resist their circumstances. Understanding the context of behaviors begins to determine the ways in which specific behaviors evolve in response to unique experiences. Revealing internal and external responses adds breadth and depth to a range of responses that includes both the covert and the overt individual experience. Finally, formulating responses as resistance confirms an ongoing and committed effort of children and youth to sustaining their safety, dignity and self-respect. It will demonstrate to professionals that these kids are responding to their circumstances rather than exhibiting symptoms of mental illness.

Throughout this book, we have viewed the system of foster care through the eyes of a child and through the eyes of an adult. Some of the key themes that have emerged include belonging, diagnosis, positive/negative social responses, and the interpretation(s) of behavior, assessment, trauma, grief and loss. As a result, we are making the following bold recommendations to all professionals connected to the foster care system within Canada and the United States. We believe these recommendations are both practical and ambitious—the goal of this project.

1. **Undertake a complete, multi-disciplinary assessment prior to a foster home placement. This assessment should not be solely focused upon the child/youth, but also on the foster home.**

    • As described in Chapter 5, we believe that this

assessment should include a multi-disciplinary team that is inclusive of current and former foster parents.

- A clearly identified process should be adopted within the government agency of each region or county.
- This assessment process should not be limited to kids entering care, but also those experiencing more than one move within a one-year period.
- This assessment process should not be limited to the 'mental health issues' of children and youth. Recognition is required of relational issues, responses and resistance, and social responses.

2. **Create adequate and qualified Emergency resources.**

- In order for the assessment process to be effective, the creation of a safe emergency placement must be created. The assessment process takes time, and kids need to be safe and stabilized during this time.
- The emergency resource must employ appropriately trained individuals in the specific areas of trauma, violence, and grief/loss. When kids are removed without notice or planning; the traumatic experience of such a disruption must be recognized and adequately addressed.
- Emergency resources are prepared for a crisis situation at all times. They are not attempting to 'adjust' emergencies into the daily/nightly functioning of family life. The youth who are 'dropped' into these situations have spoken clearly: they don't get enough attention, they are

painfully and chronically uncomfortable, and they "feel naked".

- The current practice of dropping frightened children and youth off to unprepared caregivers in the middle of the night is inadequate.

3. **Provide mandatory annual training to all foster parents for working with children and youth around issues of loss, grief and traumatic experiences.**

- Referring children and youth to a counselor will ultimately be one more loss in their lives, *if* a connection is formed with that counselor. While therapeutic services may be required, we propose that they are carefully incorporated into a 'care team' that includes relational sustainability.
- We believe that there is tremendous value in training the people who have the highest probability of staying in their lives—caregivers.
- This training must entail much more detail than understanding the definitions and theories of grief, loss and trauma. It must include information about *what to do* in the most vulnerable moments presented by children and youth.
- This is not a suggestion that other professionals will not become involved. However, we believe that the greatest potential value will come from the consistent, relational, educated support of the most committed adults in the lives of children and youth.

4. **Provide predictable support and clinical supervision to all foster parents.**

- Systemically, we propose that caregivers are often in the best position to support children and youth through issues of trauma, loss and grief due to the nature of the longer-term, trusting relationships that they form.
- Although this is not a replacement for therapeutic counselling, supporting and supervising caregivers is essential for their equal inclusion as part of the collaborative team working for children and youth.

As a society, we don't place fiscal priority on preventative measures to ensure the best possible care for the realities of children and youth in the system. We do, however, generate enough money to pick up the pieces. There is no choice but to pay for the required hospitalization, incarceration, homelessness initiatives and desperate, invasive psychiatric services. The annual estimated direct and indirect cost of child abuse and neglect in the U.S. is $103,754,017,492.00 (First Star, 2012). The information is available to us about how to 'do it right the first time'. As professionals in the field we are aware of what is not working, and we understand why. As children from the system, we are aware of the pain that we have suffered and the loss of dignity that we have endured—and we speak out.

And yet—there are nearly 100,000 children and youth in care in Canada (Youth in Care Canada, 2012) and 463,000 kids in care in the United States (National Foster Care Coalition, 2012) who are waiting for 'us' to use our collective knowledge and make the changes that we recognize are needed. They are waiting for the reallocation of funds from jails, addiction treatment programs and hospitals to the investment of preventative assessments, recruitment of qualified foster homes, and adequate training for caregivers. Collectively, we have the knowledge and individually we have the Will, otherwise we likely would not have been drawn into this field. Systemic change can occur through the stamina of individuals working in solidarity and applying their knowledge with their Will.

> Why not try to build your dream and help change the world?
>
> (Derek Clark)

Appendix 1

PSYCHOLOGICAL EVALUATION: Derek Clark

Dates Examined: 11/08/1976, 11/26/1976, 12/09/1976, 1/26/1977

Tests Administered:

Wechsler Intelligence Scale for Children (WISC)

Draw A Person (DAP)

Bender Gestalt Children's Apperception Test (CAT)

Make A Picture Story Test (MAPS)

Rorschach

Case History

"Derek was born sometime after his mother divorced her first husband. For about a year, Derek lived with his mother and biological father. It is reported that the biological father was abusive to Derek. In 1971, Derek and his mother separated from the biological father. Shortly thereafter, his mother met her present husband and remarried.

Derek's mother is the daughter of an abusive and alcoholic father. Her first husband, whom she married at age 18, was also an alcoholic and an abused child. During the marriage, a daughter was born. She is now 16 years old. Derek's father was also an alcoholic. Derek's mother's new husband is known to be very strict with children. It is not known whether or not his mother or stepfather have ever abused Derek. They have had one child together, a boy, who is three years old.

When Derek entered Kindergarten, he had a difficult time adjusting to school. His behavior was so poor that the school requested he be withdrawn from kindergarten. This past summer, his mother and stepfather took Derek to the county family services agency and requested foster home placements. The parents indicated that they had no control over Derek and could not cope with him. Derek was returned to his parents, pending a court hearing, but the parents brought him back eight days later, saying they could not control him. Since that time Derek has been in two foster homes.

In terms of his early life history, Derek was a forceps delivery and his mother had to have labor induced. There was also an Rh incompatibility. During his first year, Derek had a case of anemia. He was toilet trained at three years for urination and at four years for bowels. He has a history of temper tantrums, enuresis and encopresis. Head banging was prevalent during his second and third years and bed-wetting was frequent throughout his first five years.

Description of Behavior During Testing

Derek is a slender child of about average height and weight with brown hair and eyes. He was always neatly dressed and clean. In the waiting room, he was observed as being quiet, but once in the testing room, his behavior changed dramatically. At first, Derek was calm, but when the testing began, he became fidgety. Shortly after that, Derek became distracted and hyperactive. He did his best to avoid tasks and when he could not distract the

Examiner, he climbed all over his chair and walked around the room.

Generally, Derek responded to the Examiner in a positive mode. However, this was only after the Examiner had set limits about staying in the room and working before doing anything else. It should be noted that Derek did not always relate to the Examiner as a person. He asked her to do things for him that he did not want to do. For instance, he asked her to tie his shoe. Once, he picked up her hand and then let it go.

Every change in task caused Derek fairly severe anxiety. He would fidget or ask what time it was or tell the Examiner about his bionic powers. This behavior also occurred when the various tasks were difficult or threatening for him. At one point, the Examiner asked if he was scared and after an affirmative reply, it was discovered that Derek thought he was seeing a doctor. An explanation of the evaluation process relieved some of the anxiety, but not too much. Derek's behavior during testing appears to be fairly close to some of the reported behaviors at home and in school. Derek needed much support and encouragement to attempt the various tasks during the tests.

Intra-Test Variations:

On the WISC, Derek has a significant discrepancy between his verbal and performance scales. Derek's verbal scale indicated below average general knowledge, logical thinking and language development

Perceptual-Motor Coordinations:

In general, Derek's perceptual motor coordinations seem to be fairly good. The Bender appears to be immature. This indicates a weak visual-motor coordination. However, on coding, Derek's pencil marks are fairly age appropriate. A more likely explanation is that Derek cannot control his fine motor muscles for any length of time.

Derek's physical movements were observed to be well-coordinated and no awkwardness of movement was reported by the foster homes.

Orientation to Reality:

Throughout the testing, Derek maintained a rather tenuous reality orientation. Before the testing even began, Derek told the Examiner that he had "bionic powers," and that he wanted to be on T.V. with the "bionic man." At times, Derek seemed unable to distinguish between reality and fantasy. During the CAT Testing, he physically covered the lion on Card 3 so that the lion would not see the mouse. Derek's reality contact fluctuated among the tasks. His contact was best during the structured tasks such as PC, PA, PA, OA and the CAT. It was 1 1/2 times worse during the DAP and the Rorschach Test, which are unstructured tasks. However, Derek gave some bizarre responses during the vocabulary test which indicated that he was not staying with the situation. For instance, for "Spade," he said, "It's a spade that goes skateboarding." Most of the time, Derek's percepts were either global or fragmented. His Rorschach Test responses were global while his CAT and MAPS Tests were highly fragmented.

Qualities of Thought Processes

Derek's thought processes have a number of characteristics. Generally, Derek appears to be somewhere between the sensory-motor and the concrete state of thinking, developmentally. Derek's average math ability would indicate concrete operations. However, the numerous incidents of bizarre and fragmented thoughts make it difficult to discern his developmental level. One interesting note is that Derek has no ability to reverse thinking processes. Though Derek's verbal concept formation is very weak, his discrimination ability is fairly good. He was very observant and was able to point out and distinguish differences quickly. During the test, Derek exhibited much fantasy and delusional behavior. He also made noises that were sometimes animals and at other times were unintelligible. He appears to use his imagination as both a defense against anxiety and as a method of wish fulfillment.

Learning Process and Problem-Solving Modes:

Derek's approach to learning is a global one. He does not pursue one aspect and then another in an analytical method. He makes use of both imitation and trial and error. Even OA, his method of attack was a kind of random trial and error. He uses imitation to the extent that he could draw things that the Examiner drew first. However on BD Testing, Derek could barely copy the Examiner's demonstrations. For a six year-old, most of Derek's approaches are inadequate and immature. This is more appropriate for children aged 2 1/2 to 4 years old. Derek's DAP Test also reflects this. By six, most children are drawing whole figures. Derek could only draw a face and a sparse one at that.

His major weaknesses lay in verbal concept formation and language development. However, all of Derek's learning processes are interfered with by personality factors. He is highly anxious and is hyperactive as a result. He loses contact with reality frequently and perseverates, fantasizes and makes bizarre comments. This can happen without warning and in the middle of a task. The anxiety also manifests itself in sudden poor visual perception and in poor visual-motor coordination.

PERSONALITY ASSESSMENT Identification of Nuclear Conflicts:

The source of Derek's emotional disturbance lies within his first year of life. Even prenatally, Derek was in trouble because of the Rh factor. Then, labor had to be induced, and the baby was a forceps delivery. Also, sometime that first year, Derek was anemic and was abused by one or both parents. Therefore, the nature of his conflicts is a failure to develop any positive relationship with his mother, father or with the world. As a side effect, Derek probably was never allowed to fulfill his oral needs; at least, never in a positive, gratifying manner.

The failure to allow Derek the chance of a positive relationship with reality resulted in two things. First, he started to view the world as hostile and dangerous. Second, his helplessness in the situation caused frustration and anxiety which probably led him to withdraw. However, Derek was dependent on the environment for survival and therefore had to maintain some reality contact. This would explain Derek's severe anxiety which permeates his behavior.

In order to deal with his anxiety and growing hostility to his parents, Derek developed several defense mechanisms. He retreated into fantasy. He developed some self-stimulating behavior, which he apparently gave up after a while. He became hyperactive, because the anxiety was so overwhelming. Derek's poor relationship with his mother and his poor reality contact make new situations, such as school, threatening and anxiety provoking.

Developmental Level of Personality Development and Functioning:

Derek sees himself as weak and helpless in relation to others. As a defense against this feeling, he identifies with strong, powerful authority figures that aren't real, like the "bionic man." In view of his past history, his feeling of helplessness is probably fairly accurate. However, Derek isn't totally powerless. His eneuresis is an example of how he proves to others that they can't control him. More important, Derek became so disturbed and unmanageable that his parents got rid of him.

It is little surprise that the foster parents report that they have little problem with his behavior and that the enuresis and encopresis ceased shortly after Derek moved in with them. Since Derek has never had a positive modeling figure, this adds to his difficulties.

When Derek expresses his impulses, it is usually in terms of oral aggression, aggression in general, death or sex. All of these provoke anxiety, but the aggression provokes more anxiety than any other impulse. When he expresses an impulse fully, it is usually blunt, brief and uncensored.

For example, on Card 4 of the CAT Test, Derek plainly said that the child was going to run over his mother and kill her. This type of response triggered severe anxiety. This blunt type of response was infrequent, because Derek generally blocks his impulses and instead gives a confused and bizarre response. Derek's controls are weak and frequently give way to impulse expressions in mild or severe forms. In general, Derek's hostilities are directed toward adult authority figures and seem to be expressed more toward his mother than to his father. The impulses themselves stem from Derek's earliest phase of development.

Derek's Super-ego largely controls Derek's impulses. Because of the severe anxiety that Derek's highly punitive Super-ego metes out, Derek has a rather diffuse conscious sense of badness and worthlessness. He has internalized the idea that most of his behavior is bad and must be punished if expressed. This would be the result of early abuse and neglect. As a result, Derek developed a strict Super-ego that generally tries to prevent him from impulse expression. When Derek's impulses break through, he is punished and feels worthless. Derek's view of punishment is severe and physical, as indicated by his CAT and MAP tests. Derek's self-ideal is probably that of an omnipotent authority figure who can do anything he wants. This notion comes from Derek's fantasies of "bionic" power and his identification with superheroes.

Derek doesn't appear to be experiencing guilt for his actions. Guilt develops during the analytical phase when the child is made to feel bad, because he hasn't accomplished what his parents asked, and he wants to please them.

It is suspected that Derek never got that far in development. By the time he was a year old, Derek had probably pretty much withdrawn from reality. Then came toilet training, during which his mother forced him back into the world. She also forced him to give up a part of himself. This terrified Derek and he started having "temper tantrums" which were probably more panic reactions than actual temper tantrums.

Eventually, Derek was trained, but he continued to have bed wetting and soiling problems. Also, he didn't want to get rid of any part of himself, and as a result, he began to hold his bowel movements as long as he physically could. His foster parents discovered this behavior recently and have been able to encourage him to move his bowels regularly.

Derek's relationships with his mother and step-father are obviously poor. Derek views his parents as punitive authority figures and as devouring. The relationship was so poor that Derek ended up in a foster home. Derek likes to watch T.V. shows like "The Bionic Woman" and "The Six Million Dollar Man", and spends a good deal of his time in fantasy. No one mentioned that Derek has any interests or play activities, and this author did not observe any either, other than fantasy.

SUMMARY

Derek is a six year-old boy with "potentially" average cognitive abilities. However, his severe emotionally disturbed state of mind interferes with his overall functioning and prevents him from developing along a normal pattern. During his first year of life, Derek was the victim of child abuse. As a result of both abuse and the accompanying hostility, Derek was unable to experience a positive relationship with his mother, father or with the world. He was also unable to fulfill his oral needs in a gratifying, positive manner. Derek withdrew from reality, but maintained a tenuous relationship with it because of his dependency on it for survival. He started creating a fantasy world and developed some self-stimulating behavior.

Derek began to identify with superheroes, and currently talks of having super powers. At times, Derek seems unable to distinguish between reality and fantasy.

Derek's hostility towards his parents and especially towards his mother caused overwhelming anxiety, which Derek handled by hyperactive and regressive behavior. The strictness of Derek's parents became incorporated into his Super-ego. The Super-ego requires so much energy that Derek is virtually left without any energy for goal-directed behavior. Based on the above symptoms and facts, it is proposed that Derek has Erratic Psychosis. Immediate and prolonged play therapy is recommended. The fact that Derek still has some reality contact is a good prognostic sign if treatment is begun soon. The foster parents are willing to take Derek to therapy. It is further recommended that Derek be encouraged to identify with reality figures rather than with fantasy figures such as those on television."

SPEECH AND LANGUAGE EVALUATION July 8, 1976

"Derek was seen on July 7, 1976 for a speech and language evaluation. Referral was made because of 'gross motor problems' and his tendency to give inappropriate responses. Little was available for this child. He is currently in an emergency foster home. The home situation is chaotic.

Behavior:

The child came alone for the evaluation. He frequently requested to go home. He became restless quickly and a frequent change of activities was required, especially on difficult tasks. Cooperation was variable. At times, Derek teased and gave deliberately incorrect responses; at other times, he stated he was tired and wanted to return to his foster home.

Derek had a tendency to make hasty and often incorrect

responses, which he corrected spontaneously. Perseveration in type of responses was also noted.

Behavior was immature. Derek talked frequently about guns, knives and hurting others.

Speech and Language:

Derek's speech was intelligible. Errors on later-developing consonants were noted. The child frequently misnamed items or gave related responses before coming up with the correct words. Example: door was a window and an airport was an airplane.

When asking Derek what we cook on, he responded with bananas and food. Upon further questioning, Derek responded to the question "What do you do before crossing the street?" with "Get runned over by a car."

He initially responded to the incorrect gender (he-she) but corrected himself.

Derek has confusion of word tense and does not differentiate between today, yesterday, tomorrow.

Test Results:

Derek scored at 31 percentile for age level on the Carrow Screening Test for Auditory Comprehension of Languages. He failed concepts such as pair, coats, the girls is not swimming, the dog is in front of the car, she shows the girl the boy, the boy is chased by the dog, the man has been cutting trees, the lion has eaten, and neither the boy nor the girls is jumping.

Scores indicate that the child is "below average."

Derek cannot read, add, or identify some letters. Neurological grossly intact but IQ-performance testing is compatible with a 4 year-old.

The uniformity of the delay suggests organic "**Mild Retardation**" rather than psychosocial problems, but time will tell.

The results of this evaluation indicate that Derek would not function satisfactorily in a first grade setting. The child needs a program that would be supportive and provide success.

Recommendations:

1. Further evaluation and observation to determine the child's therapeutic and and educational needs. Derek would benefit from a complete neurological psychological assessment.

2. School placement should be carefully selected. The child needs a program where he would receive emotional support, individual help, gross and fine motor training and language therapy. This may be available through an "**educationally handicapped program**."

REPORT OF PSYCHODIAGNOSTIC EVALUATION County Mental Health Services 8/04/1976

"At the request of the County Welfare Department, a psychiatric evaluation of Derek Clark was conducted at the Guidance Clinic. The following recommendations were discussed with Derek's parents and were based upon several interviews with Derek's parents, individual play diagnostic sessions with Derek, conversations with Derek's foster mother and a review of a speech and language evaluation. Approximately 18 hours were spent in interviews and in preparation of the report.

To summarize the pertinent data, Derek is a nearly six year-old child who has been having severe behavior problems at school and in his neighborhood, to the point that his family is no longer able to cope with the pressures of complaints from neighbors and school personnel. The parents are at a loss to know how to help the boy. Derek's background includes extreme physical and economic impoverishment during infancy, and a father who brutalized the child.

Derek's mother expressed concerns that Derek's behavior

problems were a reflection of innate characteristics inherited from his natural father. The speech and language evaluation suggested the likelihood of specific learning and language problems."

"At the request of the County Welfare Department, a psychiatric evaluation of Derek Clark was conducted at the Guidance Clinic. The following recommendations were discussed with Derek's parents and were based upon several interviews with Derek's parents; individual play diagnostic sessions with Derek, conversations with Derek's foster mother and a review of a speech and language evaluation. Approximately 18 hours were spent in interviews and in preparation of the report." (Undisclosed, 1976)

Assessment of youth based solely on parent or foster parent report runs the inherent risk of bias toward an alternative agenda. "Derek's mother expressed concerns that Derek's behavior problems were a reflection of innate characteristics inherited from his natural father." (Undisclosed,1976). This may include removal of a child from the home, sedation, child-blame for behavior, etc. All assessments (medical, social worker, education) need to involve collateral sources of information. Derek's assessment did, in fact, involve people outside of his biological family. This may account for him facing minimal diagnosis (foster parents did not confirm original parent reports re: behavior) and no medication. Derek's assessment was 18 hours long; indicating collateral interviews were conducted, play diagnostic sessions were included with Derek himself, and a sufficient amount of time span was spent to ensure the context of circumstances was understood.

BIBLIOGRAPHY

Benoit, M. (2006). The View from the Mental Health System. In *Working with Traumatized Youth in Child Welfare.* New York: The Guilford Press.

Bonnah, S. (2008). *Profiles of Resistance; A Response-Based Approach with Youth in Care.* Saarbrucken: VDM Verlag.

Bowlby, J. (1989). Attachment and Loss: Volume 1. New York: Penguin Books.

Boyd Webb, N. (2006). The Impact of Trauma on Youth and Families in the Child Welfare System. In N. Boyd Webb (Ed.), *Working with Traumatized Youth in Child Welfare.* New York: The Guilford Press.

Bromfield, L. & Osborn, B. (2007). "Getting the big picture': A synopsis and critique of Australian out-of-home care research. *Child Abuse Prevention Issues , 26*, 1-39.

Brokenleg, M. (2008). Circle of Courage; Reclaiming Youth International. *Circle of Courage Foundation.* Victoria.

Cameron, M. E. (2006). Assessment of Trauma in Children and Youth. In N. B. Webb (Ed.), *Working with Traumatized Youth in Child Welfare.* New York: Guilford Press.

Child Welfare League of Canada. (n.d.). Retrieved January 18, 2012, from Child Welfare League of Canada: https://www.cwlc.ca

Clark, D. (2011, December 22). Response-Based Interview. (Bonnah, S., Interviewer)

Clark, D. (2012, January 30). Response-Based Interview. (Bonnah, S., Interviewer)

Clark, D. (2012, February 15). Response-Based Interview. (Bonnah, S., Interviewer)

Coates, L. &. Wade, A. (2007, July 26). Laguage and Violence: Analysis of Four Discursive Operations. *Springer Science + Business Media* .

Cournos, F. (2006). *City of One; a memoir.* New York: Authors Choice Press.

Cournos, F. (2002). The Trauma of Profound Childhood Loss: A personal and Professional Perspective. *Psychiatric Quarterly* , *73* (2), 145-156.

Dobratz, S. (2012). Personal Communication.

Dozier, M. (2005). Challenges of foster care. . *Attachment and Human Development* , *7* (1), 27-30.

Elliott, G. &. Kelly, K. *Medicating Young Minds: How to Know if Psychiatric Drugs Will Help or Hurt Your Child.* New York: STC Healthy Living.

First Star. (2012, March 02). *First Star.* Retrieved March 02, 2012, from http://ww.firststar.org/policy-legislation/ federal-child-welfare-oversight.aspx

Harris, G. C. (2007, May 10). Psychiatrists, Children and Drug

Industry's Role. New York.

Jenkins, A. (1990). *Invitations to Responsibility; The therapeutic engagement of men who are violent and abusive.* Adelaide: Dulwich Centre.

Kubler-Ross, E. &. Kessler, D. (2005). On Grief and Grieving: Finding the Meaning of Grief Through the Five Stages of Loss. New York: Scribner.

Lambe, Y. (2009). *Drugs In our System; An Exploratory Study of The Chemical Management of Canadian Systems Youth.* Ottawa: The National Youth In Care Network.

Lambe, Y. (2006). The Chemical Management of Canadian Systems Youth. National Youth in Care Network.

Lendrum, S. &. Syme, G. (2004). Gift of Tears; A practical approach to loss and bereavement in counselling and psychotherapy. New York: Brunner-Routledge.

McParland, K. (2012). Personal Communication.

Ministry of Children and Family Development. (2012, January 13). *Ministry of Children and Family Development.* Retrieved January 13, 2012, from http://www.gov. bc.ca/mcf/

Moss, S. &. Moss, M, (1973). Separation as a Death Experience. *Child Psychiatry and human Development, 3* (3), 187-195.

National Foster Care Coalition. (n.d.). Retrieved March 18, 2012, from National Foster Care Coalition: http:// www.nationalfostercare.org/fostercare.php

Perry, B. &. Szalavitz, M. (2006). *The Boy Who Was Raised As A Dog; And Other Stories From a Child Psychiatris's Notebook.* New York: Perseus Books.

Perry, B. &. Hambrick, E.(2008). The Neurosequential Model of Therapeutics. *Reclaiming children and youth , 17* (3), 38-43.

Perry, B. (2006). Applying Principles of Neurodevelopment to Clinical Work with Maltreated and Traumatized Children; The Neurosequential Model of Therapeutics. In N. B. Webb (Ed.), *Working with Traumatized Youth in Child Welfare.* New York: The Guilford Press.

Representative For Children and Youth & Office of the Provincial Health Officer. (2009). *Kids, Crime, and Care. Health and Well-Being of Children in Care: Youth Justice Experiences and Outcomes.* Victoria: Provincial Government.

Reynolds, V. (2010). *Doing Justice As A Path To Sustainability In Community Work.* (doctoral dissertation).

Richardson, C. &. Reynolds, V. (2012). "Here We Are, Amazingly Alive".: Holding Ourselves Together with an Ethic of Social Justice in Community Work. *International Journal of Child, Youth and Family Studies , 1,* 1-19.

Richardson, C., Wade, A, & Bonnah, S. (2012). *The Medicine Wheel of Responses; Youth in Care.* Unpublished.

"Sarah". (2009, April 18). Retrieved April 18, 2009, from

National Youth In Care Network: http://www. nationalyouthincare.ca/

Seita, J. (2005). Kids Without Family Priviledge: Mobilizing Youth Development. *Reclaiming Children and Youth*, *14* (2).

Sherperis, C. R.-M. (2003). In-Home Treatment of Reactive Attachment Disorder in a Therapeutic Foster Care System: A Case Example. *Journal of Mental Health Counselling*, *25* (1), 76-88.

Stefanakis, H. (2000). Understanding and Facilitating Change For Men Who Are Violent. *Bridging the Gaps.* Vancouver.

Tarren-Sweeney, M. (2010). It's time to re-think mental health services for children in care, and those adopted from care. *Clinical Child Psychology & Psychiatry*, *15* (4), 613-26.

The Committee on Integrating the Science of Early Childhood Development. (2000). (S. &. Shonkoff, Editor) Retrieved February 3rd, 2012, from The National Academics Press: http://www.nap.edu/openbook. php?record.id=9824

The Pew Charitable Trusts. (n.d.). Retrieved January 18, 2012, from The Pew Charitable Trusts: https://www. pewtrusts.org/our_work_report_detail.aspx?id=22334

Ullman, S. (2000). Social Reaction, Coping Strategies, and Self-Blame Attributions in Adjustment to Sexual Assault. *Psychology of Women Quarterly*, *24*, 257-271.

Ullman, S. (2010). *Talking about Sexual Assault: Society's Response to Survivors.* New York: American Psychological Association.

Wade, A. & Adams, B. (n.d.). Response-Based Interviewing with victims of Violent Crimes. Unpublished Article.

Wade, A. &. Bonnah, S. (2012). Response-Based Questions. Unpublished.

Wade, A. (2007). Despair, Resistance, Hope: Response-Based Therapy with Victims of Violence. *Therapeutic Conversations.* Vancouver.

Wade, A. (2005). Objects or Agents: Contrasting Effects-Based and Response-Based Repertoires. City University of Seattle.

Wade, A. (1997). Small Acts of Living: Everyday resistance to violence and other forms of oppression. *Journal of Contemporary Family Therapy, 19,* 23-40.

Whitaker, R. (2002). *Mad in America: Bad science, bad medicine, and the enduring mistreatment of the mentally ill.* Cambridge, MA: Perseus Books.

Worden, W. (2002). Grief Counselling and Grief Therapy. New York: Springer Publishing Company.

Yalom, I. (2003). *The Gift of Therapy; An Open Letter to a New Generation of Therapists and Their Patients.* New York: HarperCollins.

Youth in Care Canada. (2012, February 27). *Youth in Care Canada.* Retrieved February 27, 2012, from http://youthincare.ca/people/

Response-Based Training Opportunities

Training With Authors Derek Clark & Shelly Bonnah, MA

DEREK CLARK and SHELLY BONNAH provide training and professional development to groups who are interested in further exploring the ideas presented within this book. The training is a combination of exploring stark realities of growing up in the system with the innovative approach of Response-Based ideas applied to working for children and youth. This training is highly interactive, informative, and entertaining—it will build the capacity of professionals committed to the lives of children and youth.

Disable the Label has been designed as a template for what we offer in our training seminars:

- ➤ Through the Eyes of a Child
- ➤ Through the Eyes of An Adult
- ➤ Who Am I & Where Do I Belong?
- ➤ Some Response-Based Ideas
- ➤ The Assessment Lens
- ➤ Watch Your Language; Words that Kill the Spirit
- ➤ Mad & Sad; Grief understood as behavior disorders
- ➤ Leadership (for Youth)

For further information contact

Derek Clark:
E-mail: Derek@iwillnevergiveup.com
Website: www.iwillnevergiveup.com

Shelly Bonnah:
E-mail: shelly@responsebasedpractice.com
Website: www.responsebasedpractice.com